Journey's End:
A Comprehensive Guide
to End-of-Life Care
and Death Doulas

How to Do End-of-Life Better—Complete With End-of-Life Workbook (Everything You Need to Know About End-of-Life)

Georgina Solomou

Table of Contents

TRIGGER WARNING: THIS BOOK CONTAINS INFORMATION ABOUT DEATH.

Introduction

Facing the end of life is one of the most challenging experiences we can encounter. Whether it's coming to terms with a terminal diagnosis or witnessing the decline of physical or mental abilities, these moments can feel overwhelming. However, navigating this journey with compassion and a sense of empowerment can profoundly impact the quality of the experience for everyone involved.

Experiencing the end of life is incredibly personal and differs greatly from person to person. This journey is significantly shaped by age, cultural background, and the type of prognosis—whether abrupt and frightening or gradual and predictable over an extended length of time. While acknowledging one's own mortality can cause some people to feel at ease and embrace it, it can also cause concern and unanswered questions in others. Some people can even be in denial, finding it difficult to acknowledge the inevitable and often avoiding important conversations that can help them and their loved ones prepare for the final stages of life.

Putting these differences aside, there is one basic human need that never goes away: the urge to be loved and feel supported. This support can take many forms, ranging from helpful advice on everyday issues to emotional support and spiritual direction. It's important to understand that what comforts one person may not always soothe another. Thus, providing compassionate end-of-life care requires recognizing various coping processes and individual choices.

During end-of-life care, death doulas play a crucial role, shedding light on the journey ahead and creating a space for reflection, exploration, and preparation. As guides, they provide emotional, spiritual, and practical support to you and your loved ones, helping you understand and come to terms with the inevitable and find peace amid uncertainty. The workbook invites you to engage in deep introspection, conversations, and rituals that honor life and acknowledge the reality of death. Through storytelling, legacy work, advance care planning, and other transformative practices, this book enables you to confront your fears, express your wishes, and shape the narrative of your own end-of-life journey with the assistance of a death doula.

In essence, a death doula sets the stage for a meaningful and dignified passage, blending guidance with introspection, compassion with empowerment, and acceptance with preparation. Embracing the role of a death doula in end-of-life care can be a deep and enriching experience, offering a holistic approach to the inevitable voyage we all must undertake.

By reading this book, you will gain a deeper understanding of living toward the end of life and learn to accept your own mortality. This guide provides clear instructions on how to have meaningful conversations with your loved ones about death, make well-informed end-of-life decisions, and find stability in the midst of loss.

The presence of death doulas has the power to turn the often frightening end-of-life experience into a significant period of reflection and bonding. I began providing end-of-life care many years ago, driven both by my professional training and my own personal experience.

Helping people and families through the dying process has given me unique insights and practical experience, which I am sharing with you now. My goal is to provide sincere and compassionate support based on years of personal experience. This book's core is this synthesis of knowledge and compassion, which gives you both useful skills and emotional support.

I chose to write this book because I have real-life experience and understand the many challenges faced when providing end-of-life care. Having a solid foundation in business, psychology, nutritional medicine, and health science, I unexpectedly acted as a death doula in the end-of-life care for both of my parents. This led me down the path of looking for death doulas and studying how they play a role in the dying process. My life experiences and being a mother of five adult children have given me a deep sense of empathy and an appreciation for the significance of discussing difficult subjects, especially those related to death and grief.

For the past decade, I have dedicated myself to caring for my aging parents, navigating the complexities of dementia and stroke with grace and determination. I ensured their final years were filled with dignity and love, advocating fiercely for their wishes amid societal pressures and medical interventions. Despite the challenges, I created a nurturing environment where my parents could spend their final moments surrounded by family and love.

The untimely suicide of my children's father profoundly altered the course of my life. This heartbreaking experience solidified my conviction about the importance of acceptance and honest communication, particularly regarding end-of-life issues. It underscored for me the need to address difficult topics openly, to seek support, and to foster understanding and compassion within families. Currently, I am dedicated to caring for my sister, who is living with congestive heart failure. Together, we are making the most of our time, actively engaging in meaningful experiences and ticking off items on her bucket list. We have candid conversations about her final wishes, ensuring that we both feel heard and understood. This journey has taught me the immense value of living fully in the present while preparing thoughtfully for the future. Through these experiences, I have learned that embracing life's fragility with openness and love can transform even the most challenging moments into opportunities for connection and growth. I am hoping that my narrative exhibits the strength of empathy, compassion, and resilience in negotiating life's most difficult moments. By engaging in thoughtful end-of-life planning, I have observed firsthand the sincere effect it has on people and their loved ones. This book acts as a comprehensive guide and workbook full of practical templates and exercises meant to assist you in reflecting on your values, communicating your wishes, and planning for your end-of-life care.

Engaging in these exercises will prepare you to face the future with clarity and assurance. Whether you are seeking information, caring for a loved one, or grappling with your own mortality, this book provides a secure and supportive space to address these meaningful subjects. It is an invitation to approach death with the same respect and purpose that you give to the remainder of your life, surrounded by the support and understanding that you deserve.

As you go through this book, may you find the guidance and comfort you seek, and may you feel supported in every step of your journey toward a more conscious and compassionate approach to death. The first chapter is designed to help you embrace your end-of-life experience.

Chapter 1:

Embracing the Journey

To begin to embrace the end-of-life journey, we must first understand what end-of-life means. The definition of end-of-life involves several factors from the medical, psychological, and existential domains.

From a medical perspective, the development of a terminal illness and the decline in body functioning due to illness or age frequently signal the end of life.

This stage signifies not only the end of physical life but also a significant shift marked by a wide range of emotions and challenges.

Psychologically, people facing their final days may experience a range of emotions, from acceptance and serenity to fear and denial. The existential dimension raises deep questions concerning the purpose of life, the meaning of legacy, and the essence of existence itself.

These existential questions frequently cause people to consider the meaning of their lives and the legacy they want to leave behind.

Embracing the end-of-life journey means facing these varied viewpoints head-on with bravery and reflection. It entails accepting that the end of life is inevitable while simultaneously looking for comfort and purpose in the face of uncertainty.

By embracing the physiological, psychological, and existential aspects of this journey, we can cultivate a heightened sense of acceptance and tranquility when confronted with life's most significant transition.

Embracing the journey also entails understanding how the world around us influences our views on the end of life. Throughout history, cultures and traditions have shaped our perspectives and perceptions of the final days, resulting in diverse beliefs and practices.

In ancient civilizations, living your last breath was often viewed as a natural and cyclical part of life, with rituals and ceremonies designed to honor the deceased and guide their spirits to the afterlife. In contrast, some cultures viewed living the last breath with fear and trepidation, associating it with the unknown and the supernatural.

Our perspectives on living through the final days have changed with the evolution of cultures. The emergence of organized religions brought fresh perspectives on the end of life and related customs, which influenced societal norms and behaviors. For instance, cremation and the scattering of ashes in holy rivers are important rites in Hinduism, which views the final days as a passage from this life to the next.

Similarly, Buddhism views the final days as a normal part of the cycle of rebirth and practices rituals aimed at assisting the dead in reaching enlightenment. The way that people view the last days has also notably changed over time in Western societies. Nearing the end of life was frequently associated with grief and weeping in medieval Europe when the departed were honored with ornate funeral ceremonies and processions. However, views on the final days started to shift with the advent of the scientific revolution and the Age of Enlightenment. Living through the final days was seen as a problem that needed to be solved rather than a normal aspect of life, and it became increasingly medicalized. This change paved the way for the creation of contemporary funeral customs and the medicalization of end-of-life care.

Despite these changes, many cultures and traditions continue to embrace the end of life as an inevitability, with rituals and ceremonies designed to honor the deceased and support the grieving process (Wolfelt, 2023). In Mexico, for example, Day of the Dead celebrations are held annually to honor deceased loved ones and celebrate their lives. Families gather to build altars adorned with photographs, candles, and offerings, creating a festive atmosphere that celebrates the continuity of life and the end of life (National Geographic, 2016).

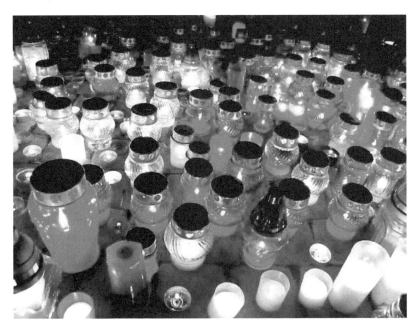

Comparably, the yearly Obon holiday in Japan is a time to pay respect to the spirits of departed family members and ancestors. Families get together to perform customary dances and ceremonies, offer prayers and incense, and clean and adorn graves. In addition to paying respect to the departed, these customs help fortify family ties and promote a feeling of community (Purwanto, 2022).

As you read further into this chapter, you will see that there is a growing movement in modern culture to reclaim the end of life as a sacred and natural aspect of life. Death doulas, who are professionals with training in holistic care and support, are part of this reclamation as they offer practical, emotional, and spiritual support to those nearing the end of life and their families during the end-of-life process.

While you will learn to understand end-of-life care in the upcoming chapter, accepting that the end of life is an inevitable aspect of existence and learning about the various cultural traditions surrounding it will help you develop a stronger sense of acceptance and peace in the face of life's most significant transition.

Defining the End of Life

As you begin to navigate the end-of-life journey, it's helpful to understand what this process entails from various perspectives. Defining the end of life involves looking at it through medical, psychological, and existential lenses. Medically, the end of life is characterized by a decline in physical health, often accompanied by the cessation of treatments aimed at curing illness or maintaining life.

Instead, the focus shifts to palliative care, which aims to provide comfort and manage symptoms to improve the quality of your final days. This approach prioritizes your comfort, ensuring you experience as little pain and distress as possible.

Psychologically, the end of life can bring a range of emotions, from fear, denial, and anxiety to acceptance and peace. It's natural to grapple with the idea of mortality and the unknown.

For many, this period is a time of reflection when they revisit their life's journey, relationships, and accomplishments. The psychological support provided by loved ones, caregivers, and professionals can play a crucial role in helping to navigate these emotions, fostering a sense of peace and acceptance.

Existentially, the end of life prompts profound questions about meaning, purpose, and what lies beyond.

Different cultures and traditions offer varied perspectives on these questions, often providing comfort and guidance. Historically, humanity's perception of the end of life has evolved, moving from a taboo topic to one that is increasingly discussed openly and with compassion.

This shift allows for more meaningful conversations about your wishes, legacies, and how you want to be remembered.

Traditions and Cultures Around End-of-Life

Exploring different cultures and traditions around the end of life can provide valuable insights into how other societies embrace this inevitable part of life. In many cultures, the end of life is not seen as an end but a transition.

As stated before, in Mexican culture, Día de los Muertos (Day of the Dead) is a celebration when families honor their deceased loved ones with altars, offerings, and festivities.

This tradition embraces the end of life as a natural part of life, promoting a sense of continuity and remembrance. Families gather to create vibrant altars adorned with marigolds, photos, and the favorite foods of the departed.

This practice honors the dead and comforts the living by reinforcing familial bonds and cultural identity.

In many Eastern traditions, such as Buddhism, the final days are viewed as a part of the cycle of life, end of life, and rebirth. These beliefs encourage individuals to live mindfully and prepare for the end with a sense of calm and acceptance.

In Buddhist philosophy, the concept of impermanence, which teaches that all things, including life, are transient, is central. This perspective helps individuals face the final days with less fear and more serenity.

Monks often chant and meditate with those nearing the end of life to provide spiritual support, helping them achieve a peaceful state of mind that facilitates a better rebirth (University of Bristol, 2023).

Similarly, in Hinduism, the belief in reincarnation shapes attitudes toward the last days, with rituals designed to aid the soul's journey to its next life. Hindus perform elaborate rites known as Antyesti, or the last sacrifice, which typically includes bathing the body, dressing it in new clothes, and cremation. The ashes are then often immersed in a sacred river, such as the Ganges, to purify the soul. These rituals underscore the importance of detachment from the physical body and the belief in an eternal soul that transitions to a new existence (Britannica, 2023).

In some African cultures, the last days are seen as a reunion with ancestors, and elaborate funerals are held to celebrate the deceased's life and ensure a smooth transition to the afterlife. The mourning period can be extensive, allowing the community to express grief and support the bereaved. In Ghana, for instance, funerals are grand affairs with music, dancing, and storytelling that honor the deceased's life and accomplishments. The Ashanti people believe in the concept of Sunsum, a spiritual essence that continues to exist after the end of life and influences the living. These funerals serve as both a farewell and a means to maintain harmony between the living and the dead (Ekore & Lanre-Abass, 2016).

In Tibetan culture, the practice of sky burial, where the deceased's body is offered to vultures, exemplifies a profound connection to nature and the belief in the impermanence of the body. This ritual is both practical, given the rocky terrain unsuitable for burial, and deeply spiritual, reflecting the Buddhist belief in the cycle of life and the transference of merit. The sky burial is a final act of generosity, providing sustenance to other living beings, and symbolizes the soul's release from the physical form (Woaber, 2022).

In Japan, the practice of Mizuko Kuyo, a ceremony to honor stillborn, miscarried, or aborted children, reflects a compassionate approach to grief and loss. Parents offer prayers, toys, and small statues to Jizo, the Buddhist guardian of children, seeking forgiveness and peace. This ritual provides a space for mourning and reconciliation, acknowledging the emotional impact of loss and fostering healing (Prichep, 2015).

In contrast to these spiritual and ritualized approaches to the end of life, Western cultures often emphasize medical intervention and prolonging life, sometimes at the expense of its quality. While in the past, Western attitudes toward death were more communal, with home funerals and wakes being common, the professionalization of end-of-life care over time has led to a more clinical approach to the final days.

However, there is a growing movement toward accepting the end of life as natural, with an increasing focus on palliative care and hospice services that prioritize comfort and dignity. There has also been a resurgence in home funerals and end-of-life-positive movements, which advocate for open discussions about end-of-life and living through the final days. These movements aim to demystify death and encourage people to plan for their end-of-life care in a way that aligns with their values (Aramesh, 2016).

These diverse perspectives and practices highlight that the quest to find meaning and comfort in the face of the end of life is universal. By understanding and integrating these cultural insights, you can approach the end of life with greater wisdom and compassion. As these traditions illustrate, embracing the inevitability of experiencing the end of life allows you to live more fully and prepare for the transition with a sense of peace and acceptance.

Medical Interventions and Embracing End-of-Life

Medical intervention at the end of life often focuses on palliative care, which aims to provide relief from the symptoms and stress of serious illness. This care can include pain management, assistance with daily activities, and emotional support. The goal is to improve the quality of life for both the person nearing the end of life and their family.

Palliative care and end-of-life care are two interconnected concepts that often overlap but possess distinct focuses. While both aim to provide comfort, support, and dignity to individuals with serious illnesses, the primary difference lies in their scope and duration.

Palliative care is a comprehensive approach that prioritizes alleviating the physical, emotional, and spiritual suffering of patients with serious illnesses, regardless of their prognosis. This type of care can span months or even years, as it focuses on improving the patient's quality of life while they undergo treatments or manage their condition.

End-of-life care, on the other hand, specifically focuses on the final stages of life, usually the last months, weeks, or days. It involves providing compassionate, supportive care to those approaching the end of their life, often when curative treatments are no longer effective or have been discontinued.

Throughout this discussion, we will use the terms palliative care and end-of-life care somewhat interchangeably, acknowledging that they often overlap. However, it's essential to recognize that palliative care can be a long-term process, while end-of-life care is typically a more condensed, intense period of support. By understanding these nuances, we can better appreciate the importance of comprehensive care that addresses the unique needs of people with life-limiting illnesses and their loved ones during these challenging times.

Palliative care teams work collaboratively with patients, their families, and other healthcare providers to tailor care plans that respect individual wishes and needs. These teams typically consist of doctors, nurses, social workers, and chaplains who provide holistic support.

Pain management is a critical component of palliative care. It involves not only the use of medications but also nonpharmacological methods such as physical therapy, massage, and relaxation techniques. Effective pain management can significantly enhance quality of life, allowing individuals to engage more fully in their final days. Beyond physical pain, end-of-life care also addresses psychological and emotional distress, helping individuals cope with anxiety, depression, and existential concerns. This comprehensive approach ensures that the individual's overall well-being is prioritized.

Assistance with daily activities is another vital aspect of palliative care. As physical capabilities decline, individuals may require help with bathing, dressing, eating, and mobility. Palliative care providers ensure these needs are met with dignity and respect, helping individuals maintain as much independence as possible. Receiving emotional support during this phase is also important. Palliative care teams offer counseling and support groups for both the individual and their loved ones, providing a safe space to express fears, hopes, and grief. This emotional care can create a more supportive and nurturing environment, fostering resilience and comfort.

It is important to have open and honest conversations with healthcare providers about your wishes and preferences for care during your final days. Advance care planning, which includes discussing and documenting your goals for care, can ensure that your wishes are respected even if you become unable to communicate them. This process might involve creating an advance directive or living will, which outlines your preferences for medical treatments and interventions. By communicating your desires clearly, you help prevent unnecessary and unwanted procedures, allowing for a more peaceful and personalized end-of-life experience.

Embracing the end of life involves recognizing it as a natural part of the human experience. It allows you to focus on what truly matters, fostering deeper connections with loved ones and creating meaningful memories. Many find that acknowledging the finite nature of life brings a greater appreciation for the present moment and strengthens relationships. This perspective encourages you to engage in open conversations with your loved ones about your hopes, fears, and wishes for the end of life. These discussions can lead to greater understanding and support, easing the emotional burden for everyone involved.

By acknowledging and preparing for the end of life, you can approach it with a sense of peace and acceptance, knowing that you have made thoughtful decisions about your care and legacy. This preparation might include organizing important documents, making funeral arrangements, and writing letters or creating memory books for loved ones. Such actions can provide a sense of control and purpose, ensuring that your final wishes are honored and you leave behind a meaningful legacy for your loved ones. Embracing the end of life also means accepting the support of others. This can include professional caregivers, friends, and family members who are there to help you navigate this journey. Accepting support can alleviate feelings of isolation and provide emotional comfort. Hospice care, in particular, offers a compassionate approach to end-of-life care as it focuses on comfort rather than cure. Hospice teams provide medical, emotional, and spiritual support, helping individuals and their families navigate the final stages of life with dignity and grace.

Ultimately, the combination of palliative care and a mindful approach to end-of-life allows for a more compassionate and individualized end-of-life experience. By prioritizing comfort, dignity, and personal wishes, you can create a final chapter that reflects the individual's values and relationships. This holistic approach not only alleviates physical suffering but also nurtures the emotional and spiritual well-being of both the individual and their loved ones.

Understanding and embracing the final days as an integral part of life can transform how you live your final days. It encourages a focus on quality of life, meaningful connections, and personal legacy, helping you approach the end with peace and acceptance. By planning ahead and engaging in open, honest conversations, you can ensure that your end-of-life experience is as fulfilling and dignified as possible. Though challenging, this journey offers an opportunity for profound growth and connection, ultimately enhancing the way you live and die.

Using the Workbook

Throughout this book, you'll find practical tools and emotional support to help you navigate this journey. The included workbook offers templates and exercises designed to help you reflect on your values, communicate your wishes, and plan for your end-of-life care. These tools will enable you to face the future with clarity and confidence, ensuring that your final days are lived with dignity and surrounded by love. The workbook is a vital part of this journey. It provides a structured approach to end-of-life planning, allowing you to systematically organize your thoughts and preferences. Each section is thoughtfully designed to guide you through the process, from reflecting on personal values and beliefs to documenting medical preferences and funeral arrangements. By completing these exercises, you create a comprehensive plan that ensures your wishes are respected and your loved ones are supported.

One of the core elements of the workbook is the emphasis on personal reflection. This involves considering your own values, beliefs, and what matters most to you in your final days. Reflecting on these aspects helps you to make informed decisions about your care and legacy. The workbook includes prompts and questions that encourage deep contemplation, helping you to articulate your desires clearly. This process not only brings clarity but also provides a sense of control and empowerment.

Many people inadvertently become death doulas, guiding their loved ones through the final stages of life. This role involves advocating for their wishes within the healthcare system, providing emotional support, and navigating the complexities of end-of-life care. Your experience in this role can be profoundly meaningful, allowing you to witness the importance of compassionate care and advocacy firsthand. The workbook supports this by offering practical tools and guidance for those who find themselves in this unintentional yet crucial role. It helps you understand the responsibilities and provides resources to ensure you are well-prepared.

As you work through the templates and journal prompts in this book, you'll find guidance on everything from documenting important information and preferences to planning meaningful rituals and legacy projects. For example, there are sections dedicated to compiling vital personal and medical information, which can be invaluable for both the individual nearing the end of their life and their caregivers. Having this information readily available can ease the burden on loved ones and ensure that medical professionals know and respect preferences.

The workbook also encourages you to think about the emotional and spiritual aspects of the end-of-life journey. This includes planning for how you want to be remembered, what kind of legacy you wish to leave, and what rituals or ceremonies would be meaningful to you.

These exercises help you to create a plan that is not only practical but also deeply personal and reflective of your individuality. Additionally, the workbook provides space for documenting conversations with loved ones and healthcare providers. Effective communication is critical in end-of-life planning, and the workbook includes tips and strategies for having these important discussions. By writing down the outcomes of these conversations, you ensure that everyone involved understands your wishes and can act accordingly. This can prevent misunderstandings and ensure that your end-of-life care is aligned with your values and preferences.

Another significant aspect of the workbook is its focus on legacy projects. These are personal endeavors that allow you to leave a lasting impact, whether through letters to loved ones, memory books, or other creative expressions. Engaging in legacy projects can be a source of comfort and fulfillment, providing a tangible way to express your love and gratitude to those who matter most. The workbook offers ideas and templates to help you get started, making it easier to create meaningful and lasting tributes.

The workbook also includes sections on managing practical considerations, such as financial planning, legal documents, and funeral arrangements. These practical aspects are often overlooked but are crucial for ensuring that your wishes are carried out smoothly. By addressing these details in advance, you relieve your loved ones of the burden of making difficult decisions during a challenging time. The workbook provides checklists and templates to help you organize these important details effectively.

By engaging in these exercises, you will be better prepared to face the future with clarity and confidence. The process of using the workbook can be therapeutic, providing a structured way to process your thoughts and feelings about the end of life. It helps to demystify the process, making it more approachable and less daunting. By taking proactive steps, you can approach your final days with a sense of peace and assurance, knowing that you have made thoughtful and intentional decisions about your care and legacy. The workbook is more than just a practical tool; it is a companion on your journey, offering support and guidance as you navigate the complexities of end-of-life planning. By embracing this resource, you can ensure that your final days are lived with dignity, surrounded by love, and reflective of your unique values and beliefs.

Self-Reflective Questions

1. How can I develop the emotional fortitude and empathy needed to provide people and their loved ones with the complete support they need throughout the deep and holy transition of end-of-life?

_____

_____

_____

_____

_____

_____

_____

_____

_____

_____

_____

_____

_____

_____

_____

_____

_____

_____

_____

_____

_____

_____

_____

_____

2. How can I create a safe and nonjudgmental space for individuals to express their emotions and concerns, and what skills do I need to develop to maintain that space?

_____

_____

_____

_____

_____

_____

_____

_____

_____

_____

_____

_____

_____

_____

_____

_____

_____

_____

_____

_____

_____

_____

_____

3. What personal experiences or losses can I draw upon to develop a deeper understanding of the grieving process, and how can I use those insights to provide more effective support?

_____

_____

_____

_____

_____

_____

_____

_____

_____

_____

_____

_____

_____

_____

_____

_____

_____

_____

_____

_____

_____

_____

4. How can I prioritize my own emotional well-being and self-care to avoid burnout, ensuring that I can sustainably provide emotional support to those in need throughout their difficult times?

_____

_____

_____

_____

_____

_____

_____

_____

_____

_____

_____

_____

_____

_____

Chapter 2:

Understanding End-of-Life Care

This chapter explores the vital topic of end-of-life care, offering insights into its many facets to help you understand what it entails and why compassionate, holistic support is crucial during this challenging time. End-of-life care takes a comprehensive approach to support individuals nearing the end of their lives, aiming to make their final days as comfortable and meaningful as possible. This includes not only managing medical symptoms but also providing emotional, spiritual, and psychological support.

One of the key components of end-of-life care is the role of death doulas, whose services provide invaluable benefits to both those reaching the end of their lives and their families. Death doulas offer personalized, nonmedical support that complements the work of other end-of-life care providers. By exploring the unique contributions of death doulas, we can appreciate how they differ from traditional healthcare professionals and the unique value they bring to the end-of-life experience.

Join me as I uncover the essential elements of end-of-life care and the transformative impact of death doulas. This chapter will equip you with a deeper understanding of how holistic end-of-life care can enhance the quality of life for those nearing the end and their loved ones, fostering a more compassionate and dignified approach to this inevitable journey.

What Is End-of-Life Care?

End-of-life care is a comprehensive strategy for assisting people to approach the end of their lives with grace, comfort, and a sense of empowerment. It includes managing a person's emotional, psychological, and spiritual aspects of their experience in addition to their physical symptoms. This holistic support system acknowledges the interdependence of the mind, body, and spirit, addressing each component to offer compassionate and well-rounded care.

The physical component of holistic end-of-life care concentrates on easing pain and managing symptoms. This could entail numerous medical interventions, integrative therapies, and drugs designed to alleviate discomfort and enhance quality of life. While meeting the physical needs of the person reaching the end of life is the central component, effective end-of-life care also addresses their emotional and psychological needs.

People who are nearing the end of life frequently feel a variety of emotions, such as fear, anxiety, sadness, and occasionally relief. Providing emotional support in the form of therapy, for instance, counseling and attentive listening, enables those facing their final days to process their feelings and find comfort.

Spiritual support is another vital component of end-of-life care, offering individuals the opportunity to explore and affirm their beliefs, seek meaning, and attain a sense of spiritual peace. This might involve religious rituals, spiritual counseling, or facilitating connections with faith leaders. Spiritual support is deeply personal and varies significantly from person to person, but it is crucial in helping individuals find solace and meaning as they approach the end of their lives. This holistic approach ensures that all aspects of a person's being are considered and respected, creating a more humane and compassionate end-of-life experience.

The Role of Death Doulas in End-of-Life Care

The introduction of death doulas, also known as end-of-life doulas, is one of the biggest advancements in end-of-life care. Death doulas provide holistic, nonmedical support to enhance the efforts of conventional healthcare providers. They concentrate on offering individualized care that attends to the emotional and spiritual needs of the person nearing the end of life and their family. By providing a constant, consoling presence that aids in navigating the complications of dying, a death doula can completely change the experience.

Death doulas provide numerous benefits to individuals and families. They offer practical assistance with tasks such as planning and coordinating end-of-life arrangements and ensuring that the individual's wishes are documented and respected. They also create a comforting environment, often facilitating a space where people reaching the end of life can reflect, share memories, and express their feelings without fear of judgment. This personalized support can significantly ease the emotional burden on both the individual and their loved ones, fostering a sense of peace and acceptance (Springhills, 2024).

Death doulas are essential for providing emotional and psychological care in addition to practical help. They offer a sympathetic presence, paying attention to the hopes, concerns, and fears of the individual who is nearing the end of life, helping them process their emotions and find solace in their last days.

A death doula's assistance can also be invaluable in helping families process their own grief and prepare for the approaching passing. By providing a soothing presence and encouraging candid discussions, death doulas assist in easing anxiety and fostering a feeling of closure for both the person nearing the end of life and their loved ones.

The nonmedical focus of death doulas sets them apart from other end-of-life care providers, such as hospice aides or palliative care physicians. Death doulas offer the compassionate, practical, and emotional support that goes hand in hand with the clinical and symptom management that medical professionals focus on.

This person-centered, holistic approach guarantees that every facet of a patient's health is taken care of. Medical experts and death doulas work together to provide a complete support system that respects the needs and desires of the individual (Springhills, 2024).

Frequently Asked Questions

The following are five commonly asked questions concerning end-of-life care and death doulas.

What is a death doula, and what role do they play in end-of-life care?

A death doula is a qualified professional who offers individuals and their families holistic, nonmedical care as they navigate their final days. They provide practical, spiritual, and emotional support to assist people facing the end of life with dignity and compassion. This role can involve a range of activities, such as helping to articulate wishes, supporting families in understanding the end-of-life process, and offering a comforting presence during the final days. Death doulas work to ensure that both the individual and their loved ones feel heard, understood, and supported. They often bridge the gap between medical professionals and family members, helping to navigate the complexities of end-of-life care and ensuring that the wishes of the individual are respected.

Death doulas also assist with the practical aspects of end-of-life, such as creating advance care plans, organizing important documents, and helping to facilitate legacy projects. They may also guide families through the process of creating meaningful rituals or ceremonies to honor the life of the deceased. In this way, death doulas provide a comprehensive support system that addresses the multifaceted needs of those nearing the end of life. Their holistic approach ensures that the emotional, spiritual, and practical dimensions of dying are all attended to, creating a more peaceful and dignified experience for everyone involved.

Additionally, death doulas often play a crucial role in educating families about the natural process of dying. They provide information on what to expect in the final days and hours, helping to alleviate fears and misconceptions. By offering continuous support and reassurance, death doulas help families feel more prepared and less overwhelmed. This educational aspect of their work is vital in fostering a sense of calm and acceptance, allowing families to focus on spending meaningful time with their loved ones (Springhills, 2024). In many cases, death doulas also provide grief support after the death of a loved one. They help families process their loss and begin the journey of healing. This ongoing support can be invaluable in helping individuals navigate the complex emotions that accompany grief. By providing a safe space for expressing sorrow and remembering the deceased, death doulas contribute to the emotional well-being of the entire family. Their presence ensures that the end-of-life experience is not only about managing death but also about celebrating life and legacy.

How is end-of-life care different from hospice care?

End-of-life care is a broader term encompassing the physical, emotional, and spiritual care provided to individuals in the final stages of life, regardless of prognosis. Hospice care, on the other hand, is a specific type of end-of-life care that focuses on providing comfort and support to individuals with a terminal illness. This type of care aims to support the individual and their family through the complexities of the end-of-life process, ensuring that their needs and wishes are met with respect and compassion.

Hospice care, on the other hand, is a specific type of end-of-life care that focuses on providing comfort and support to individuals with a terminal illness. This type of care is generally reserved for those who have been given a prognosis of six months or less to live and who have decided to forgo curative treatments. Hospice care prioritizes pain management and symptom relief, aiming to provide the highest quality of life possible in the time remaining. This care model is holistic, addressing not just the physical aspects of the illness but also the emotional, spiritual, and social needs of the patient and their family.

A key distinction between hospice care and broader end-of-life care is the approach to treatment. While end-of-life care may still involve curative or life-prolonging treatments depending on the person's wishes and medical condition, hospice care focuses exclusively on palliative care. This means that all efforts are directed toward comfort and quality of life rather than attempting to cure the illness. Hospice care teams typically include a variety of healthcare professionals, such as doctors, nurses, social workers, chaplains, and trained volunteers, all working together to provide comprehensive support. Furthermore, hospice care often includes additional services such as respite care for family caregivers, bereavement support for loved ones after death, and assistance with practical matters like advance care planning and funeral arrangements. By offering a coordinated, multidisciplinary approach, hospice care aims to ease the burden on families and ensure that the final days of a person's life are as peaceful and meaningful as possible.

This specialized focus on terminal care distinguishes hospice from the broader spectrum of end-of-life care, which may encompass a wider array of treatment options and support services depending on the individual's condition and preferences.

What services do death doulas typically provide?

Death doulas provide a variety of services, such as providing emotional support to the individual and their loved ones, helping with legacy projects and life reviews, offering guidance on advance care planning, helping with funeral arrangements, and establishing a calm and sacred environment for the dying process.

They assist individuals with reflecting on their lives and creating meaningful mementos for loved ones. This might include recording personal stories, writing letters, or organizing photo albums.

Additionally, death doulas offer guidance on advance care planning, helping individuals to articulate their wishes regarding medical treatments and end-of-life care. This planning ensures that their preferences are respected and reduces the burden on family members.

Another critical service provided by death doulas is assistance with funeral arrangements. They can coordinate with funeral homes, help select meaningful rituals, and support the family in creating a ceremony that honors the individual's life and beliefs.

By establishing a calm and sacred environment, death doulas help those nearing the end of life to experience peace and comfort. This may involve the use of music, aromatherapy, and other soothing practices tailored to the individual's preferences.

Here is a testimonial from Claire, whose mother was cared for by a death doula:

"When my mother was nearing the end of her life, we were blessed to have a death doula by our side. Her support was invaluable. She helped us create a memory book filled with my mother's stories and photographs, something we will cherish forever. The doula also guided us through advance care planning, ensuring my mother's wishes were clearly documented and respected.

She coordinated with the funeral home and helped us plan a beautiful service that truly reflected my mother's spirit. The atmosphere she created in my mother's final days was incredibly peaceful, filled with soft music and the gentle scent of lavender. Her presence provided us with comfort and strength during a very difficult time."

How can a death doula help with grief and bereavement?

Death doulas provide emotional support and companionship to individuals and families as they navigate the grieving process. They offer a listening ear, validation of feelings, and guidance on coping strategies to help individuals process their grief and adjust to life after loss.

One crucial way death doulas assist with grief and bereavement is by creating a safe space for individuals nearing the end of life and their families to express their emotions openly and without judgment. This can include facilitating meaningful conversations about memories, fears, and hopes for the future.

By acknowledging and validating these emotions, death doulas help individuals feel understood and supported during a time of profound transition.

Additionally, death doulas offer practical guidance on coping strategies for grief. This may involve recommending therapeutic techniques such as journaling, mindfulness exercises, or connecting with support groups. By providing these tools, death doulas empower individuals to navigate their grief journey with resilience and self-awareness.

Here is a testimonial from Robert, whose wife received support from a death doula:

"As my wife approached the end of her life, we were fortunate to have a compassionate death doula to help us navigate through the process. She provided not only physical care but also emotional support, which was invaluable during such a difficult time. After my wife passed away, the doula continued to check in with me regularly, offering a listening ear and practical advice on managing grief. Her presence helped me to process my emotions and find moments of peace amid the overwhelming sadness. I will always be grateful for her guidance and support during one of the darkest periods of my life."

Are death doulas only for individuals who are actively dying?

Death doulas can assist individuals and their families from diagnosis to the time of death, as well as throughout the entire journey of the end-of-life process. The end-of-life process from diagnosis to final days can range from days, weeks, months, or sometimes even years. Having someone to help navigate these stages and challenges is essential in providing a more manageable and caring end-of-life experience. Sometimes, the person reaching the end of life has accepted the inevitability of their situation, but their family members are in denial, unwilling to accept the diagnosis, and wanting to only "talk positive." In these cases, it is the role of death doulas to offer vital support to help them and their families and caregivers overcome the difficulties and feelings associated with approaching end-of-life.

Death doulas provide continuous emotional and practical support throughout the end-of-life journey. From the moment of diagnosis, death doulas can help patients and their families come to terms with the prognosis, understand treatment options, and make informed decisions about care preferences. This early involvement allows for a more holistic approach to end-of-life planning, ensuring that the individual's wishes and values are honored throughout their journey. For instance, Sarah's experience with a death doula began shortly after her father's terminal cancer diagnosis. The doula supported the family in understanding the progression of the disease, discussing treatment goals, and preparing for the inevitable changes in her father's condition. As Sarah's father moved through different stages of illness, the doula provided emotional reassurance and practical advice on symptom management and comfort care. This continuous support not only helped alleviate Sarah's anxiety but also empowered her family to focus on creating meaningful moments together during her father's final months. The emergence of death doulas reflects a broader shift toward a more compassionate and comprehensive approach to end-of-life care. This approach recognizes that dying is a profound life event that deserves dignity, respect, and personalized support. By integrating emotional, spiritual, and physical care, death doulas contribute to creating a more comforting and meaningful experience for individuals nearing the end of life and their loved ones.

Death doulas bring unique qualities and skills to the end-of-life care team. They are trained to provide compassionate companionship, actively listen to concerns, and offer guidance on navigating the healthcare system. Their presence can help alleviate fear and uncertainty, foster open communication within families, and ensure that the wishes of those under their care are communicated and respected. By advocating for the individual's needs and preferences, death doulas play a crucial role in enhancing the quality of life in the final stages.

In summary, death doulas are not limited to providing support only to those actively dying but are instrumental in offering guidance and comfort throughout the entire end-of-life journey. Their role extends from diagnosis through to death and into bereavement support for families. By embracing the services of a death doula early in the process, individuals and their families can benefit from comprehensive care that enhances dignity, comfort, and peace of mind during one of life's most challenging transitions.

When contemplating the process of end-of-life care, it is critical to acknowledge the importance of an all-encompassing methodology. Individuals' physical, emotional, spiritual, and practical needs can all be met to facilitate a more compassionate and well-rounded experience. The use of death doulas in this process emphasizes how crucial it is to have individualized, nonmedical support in addition to standard treatment. By fostering a more humane and dignified experience for all parties involved, this collaborative, holistic approach to end-of-life care helps people navigate the complications of dying with grace and compassion. You can learn about the duties of a death doula in Chapter 3.

Self-Reflective Questions

1. How can I acknowledge and validate the emotional struggles that individuals and their loved ones may face during the end-of-life journey while also offering reassurance and hope?

_____

_____

_____

_____

_____

_____

_____

_____

_____

_____

_____
_____
_____
_____
_____
_____
_____
_____
_____
_____
_____
_____
_____
_____
_____
_____

2. What measures can I take to ensure that the physical, emotional, and spiritual needs of individuals are being met during the end-of-life transition, and how can I adapt my support to their unique circumstances?

_____
_____
_____
_____
_____
_____
_____
_____
_____
_____
_____
_____
_____
_____
_____
_____
_____
_____
_____

3. In what ways can I create a sense of control and autonomy for individuals nearing the end of life, allowing them to make informed decisions about their care and support options?

_____
_____
_____
_____
_____
_____
_____
_____
_____
_____
_____
_____
_____
_____
_____
_____
_____
_____
_____
_____
_____
_____

4. How can I prepare myself to navigate the complex emotional landscape of grief and loss that often accompanies end-of-life care and provide sustainable support to those who are grieving?

_____
_____
_____
_____
_____
_____
_____
_____

Chapter 3:

The Role of a Death Doula

Death doulas are essential to the end-of-life care process because they provide a special kind of practical, emotional, and spiritual support to those who are nearing the end of their lives as well as their loved ones.

Death doulas, in contrast to conventional medical practitioners, concentrate on the nonmedical aspects of dying, making sure that the last days of life are spent in comfort, dignity, and meaning.

Their work is grounded in empathy and a profound comprehension of the human condition, offering a comprehensive approach that caters to the many requirements of the people they assist (Springhills, 2024).

What Do Death Doulas Do?

One of the primary roles of a death doula is to provide emotional support. Facing the end of life can evoke a wide range of emotions, including fear, denial, sadness, anger, and sometimes even relief. Death doulas offer a compassionate presence, helping individuals process these feelings and find peace. They also support family members, who often experience their own emotional turmoil as they navigate the impending loss of a loved one. By providing a calming and understanding presence, death doulas help alleviate anxiety and foster a sense of connection and closure (Springhills, 2024).

Another crucial component of a death doula's role is providing practical support. This can involve aiding with advance care planning, liaising with healthcare providers, and supporting last arrangements, including funeral planning.

Additionally, death doulas see to it that the setting is comforting and supportive of a tranquil dying process. This could entail making sure that comfort measures are in place, encouraging visits from loved ones, and setting up the physical environment to suit the individual's preferences.

The best way to fully comprehend the importance of death doulas may be through case studies and testimonials from real people who have benefited from their services. Consider the story of James, a senior citizen from Washington, D.C., who was diagnosed with terminal cancer. James was overcome with fear and anxiety over his final days, but as a death doula, Sandy spent time getting to know him, understanding his concerns, and having conversations with him about his plans. She facilitated conversations between James and his family to ensure that his desires for his final care were honored. Sandy's solace and companionship also assisted James in discovering peace and acceptance. After James's passing, his family expressed their gratitude for Sandy and how she improved their experience by adding purpose and making a difficult time more bearable.

The experience of Linda from Georgia, whose mother Margaret was nearing the end of her life after her battle with Alzheimer's disease, serves as another illustration. Caring for her dying mother presented Linda with emotional and practical hurdles that left her feeling lost and overwhelmed. Grace, a death doula, intervened and provided direction and encouragement. She arranged care with medical specialists, supported Linda emotionally, and assisted Linda in navigating the healthcare system. Because of Grace's assistance, Linda was able to spend quality time with her mother and make treasured memories during Margaret's last days. Later on, Linda conveyed her sincere gratitude for Grace's assistance, calling it a lifeline through one of the most trying times in her life.

The testimonials of those who have worked with death doulas underscore their profound impact. Families often speak of the deep sense of relief and comfort they felt, knowing that their loved one's final wishes were being honored and that they were not alone in their grief. Individuals facing the end of life express gratitude for the compassionate presence and emotional support that death doulas provide, helping them face their final days with dignity and peace.

Death doulas set themselves apart from other providers of end-of-life care with their individualized and comprehensive approach. Death doulas concentrate on the practical, emotional, and spiritual needs of those nearing the end of life and their families, while hospice and palliative care staff handle medical symptoms.

This supplementary care guarantees a comprehensive end-of-life experience, attending to every facet of an individual's welfare.

Case Study: The Story of Peter and His Family

Peter, a resident of Northern California, was diagnosed with terminal cancer. His family, overwhelmed by the emotional and logistical challenges of his diagnosis, sought the help of a death doula named Grace to navigate Peter's end-of-life journey.

From the beginning, Grace prioritized understanding Peter's personal wishes and concerns. She spent hours talking with him, learning about his fears, hopes, and the legacy he wanted to leave behind. This initial phase was crucial as it set the foundation for a relationship based on trust and empathy. Grace's presence provided Peter with a safe space to express his emotions openly, which significantly alleviated his anxiety about the future.

Grace facilitated family discussions, ensuring everyone had a chance to express their feelings and concerns. This support helped Peter and his family come to terms with the reality of his condition, reducing anxiety and fostering a sense of peace and acceptance. Grace encouraged open communication, helping the family address unresolved issues and strengthen their bonds during this challenging time.

In addition to emotional support, one of Grace's essential roles was assisting with advance care planning. She guided Peter through the process of documenting his end-of-life wishes, ensuring that his preferences were clearly outlined and respected. This included decisions about medical interventions, pain management, and personal comfort measures.

Grace's expertise in advance care planning provided Peter and his family with clarity and peace of mind, knowing that his wishes would be honored. Grace coordinated with healthcare providers to manage Peter's symptoms and maintain his comfort. She advocated for his needs, ensuring that his pain was effectively managed and that he received the best possible care. Grace's involvement in the medical aspects of Peter's care relieved his family of much of the logistical stress, allowing them to focus on spending quality time with him. Grace also played a significant role in helping the family make funeral arrangements that reflected Peter's desires. She guided them through the process, offering practical advice and emotional support.

By handling many of the details, Grace allowed the family to be present with Peter during his final days rather than being bogged down by planning and logistics.

Creating a peaceful and supportive environment for Peter's final days was another critical aspect of Grace's work. She transformed Peter's home into a tranquil space that promoted comfort and dignity. This included setting up a comfortable bed, arranging for soothing music, and displaying cherished photographs and mementos.

Grace's attention to these details created a sense of sanctuary for Peter, allowing him to spend his last moments in a setting filled with love and comfort.

Peter's family expressed profound gratitude for Grace's support. They highlighted how her presence brought a sense of calm and structure to an otherwise chaotic time. Grace's guidance allowed them to focus on spending quality time with Peter, creating lasting memories, and facilitating a smoother grieving process after his passing. The emotional support Grace provided to Peter's family was invaluable.

She helped them navigate their own feelings of grief and loss, offering a compassionate presence and a listening ear. By validating their emotions and providing coping strategies, Grace helped the family manage their grief and find a sense of closure.

When asked about their experience, the Johnson family had this to say: "Grace's support was invaluable. She helped us navigate the toughest period of our lives with compassion and expertise. Thanks to her, we were able to honor Peter's wishes and ensure his final days were filled with love and dignity. We couldn't have done it without her."

Death doulas like Grace play a crucial role in end-of-life care by providing comprehensive support that addresses emotional, practical, and spiritual needs.

Their involvement not only improves the quality of life for individuals nearing the end of their lives but also provides much-needed support and guidance to their families.

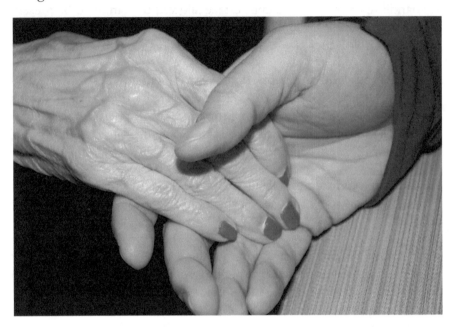

As you dig deeper into the idea of end-of-life care, remember the vital service that death doulas provide. Their all-encompassing care, which is based on compassion and understanding, adds a vital level of support that improves the dying process overall.

Whether you are coping with your own mortality, providing care for a loved one, or trying to gain a better understanding of the dying process, acknowledging the significance of death doulas can provide great understanding and solace.

Their support and presence serve as a monument to the strength of compassion throughout some of life's most trying times. The following chapter will discuss the dying process.

Self-Reflective Questions

1. How can I best honor and respect the unique wishes, beliefs, and values of those nearing the end of life while also navigating the complexities of providing compassionate and empowering support as a death doula?

_____

_____

_____

_____

_____

_____

_____

_____

_____

_____

_____

_____

_____

_____

_____

_____

_____

_____

_____

_____

_____

_____

_____

_____

2. How can I create a personalized support plan that respects the autonomy and decision-making capacity of the individual while also involving their loved ones in the process, if desired?

_____

_____

_____

_____

_____

_____

_____

_____

_____

_____

_____

_____

_____

_____

_____

_____

_____

_____

_____

3. What strategies can I use to navigate potential conflicts between the individual's wishes and the expectations of their family or caregivers, ensuring that everyone's needs are respected?

_____

_____

_____

_____

_____

_____

_____

_____

_____
_____
_____
_____
_____
_____
_____
_____
_____
_____
_____
_____
_____
_____
_____

4. In what ways can I use active curiosity and open-ended questions to uncover the unique values, beliefs, and priorities of the individual and incorporate those into their end-of-life care and support?

_____
_____
_____
_____
_____
_____
_____
_____
_____
_____
_____
_____
_____
_____
_____
_____
_____
_____
_____

Chapter 4:

The Journey Toward the Final Days

The path toward the end of life is a profound and intricate experience that encompasses spiritual, emotional, and bodily aspects. It is imperative to grasp each of these aspects to provide comprehensive support to individuals nearing the end of their lives. By acknowledging the physical changes that occur, listening to their emotional and spiritual needs, and using a range of techniques and rituals, we can help individuals approaching the end of their lives find peace and comfort.

Support systems, such as family, friends, and caretakers, are also crucial aspects of the journey toward the final days, as they are essential for offering companionship, emotional support, and a feeling of community. Understanding the importance of these relationships and reinforcing them is critical for providing meaningful support.

Open communication, active listening, and empathy between those nearing the end of life and their support systems can help everyone feel heard, validated, and loved during this difficult time. For example, in Maria's hospice room, her family made a "love wall" and placed pictures, notes, and other keepsakes from her loved ones on it. Maria felt so much comforted by this gesture as it served as a constant reminder of the love and support that was all around her.

Making sure individuals nearing the end of their lives have access to worthwhile experiences and activities can also make their final days happier and more meaningful. This could be anything from simply indulging in a favorite dish or pastime to engaging in music therapy or aromatherapy. By embracing the complex and multi-faceted nature of the end-of-life experience, we can offer complete assistance that meets the physical, emotional, and spiritual requirements of individuals facing end-of-life.

The Physical Dimensions of Dying

Understanding the physical aspects of the dying process can help those facing the end of life and their loved ones on their journey. When death is near, the body starts to shut down, and a number of physical changes occur. While each person may experience these changes differently, frequent symptoms include altered breathing patterns, a general deterioration in physical strength and mobility, and decreased hunger and thirst.

In end-of-life care, effective pain management is crucial to ensuring a person's comfort and dignity. While pain management options and preferences should have been discussed before these major physical changes occur, people may change their minds. Some people who may not have initially wanted pain management can choose it if their pain becomes unmanageable without intervention. These include pharmaceutical and nonpharmacological interventions, such as massage and relaxation techniques. Caregivers and loved ones play an essential role in the final journey, offering consolation and emotional support during the physical transition for those confronting the end of life.

It's critical to establish a calm atmosphere while honoring their individuality and culture. Physical touch, such as holding the individual's hand, playing their favorite music, or keeping family photos close by, can instill a sense of peace and tranquility and ease their passing. People who are nearing the end of their lives may also find comfort in spiritual assistance, such as prayer or religious rites. A prime example is the tale of Margaret, a devoted Catholic. She found much comfort and serenity in the regular visits from her priest, who gave her communion and said prayers.

Attending to the psychological and emotional needs of the person reaching the end of life can also alleviate the physical burden. This can reduce fear and anxiety, helping them concentrate on spending time with their loved ones. They can feel heard and supported during this crucial stage if you encourage open communication, listen to their worries, and validate their emotions. For example, John, who was having a hard time accepting his imminent death, was able to achieve closure when his family and caretakers listened to his worries and acknowledged his feelings.

The physical needs of someone nearing the end of their life can also be respected and fulfilled with the help of advance care planning. Conversations about values, wishes, and preferences, such as organ donation, life-sustaining therapies, and funeral plans, are a few examples of this. By being part of these decisions, those on the end-of-life journey can feel more in control of their circumstances and ready for the inevitable.

Attending to Emotional and Spiritual Needs

Aside from the physiological changes, major emotional and spiritual challenges are frequently encountered during the dying process. People can feel a variety of emotions, such as sadness, denial, acceptance, fear, rage, and grief. It's critical to create a secure and encouraging space where these emotions can be discussed and explored. It's also vital to encourage open and caring communication so that people may express their needs and fears without feeling judged.

In addition to reducing anxiety, this emotional support can promote empathy and understanding.

Another essential component of end-of-life care is attending to spiritual needs. When someone gets closer to the end of their life, they could look back on their life and their views about what comes after in order to find meaning and purpose in it. While some find comfort in nature, art, or introspection, others may find it by participating in religious rites and practices.

It is critical to respect each person's distinct spiritual journey and to provide them the chance to investigate and articulate their beliefs. This might involve setting up visits with spiritual leaders, creating a quiet place for them to ponder or pray, or just being there for them as they go through their last days.

Music therapy is another powerful tool for providing emotional and spiritual support. Listening to favorite songs or soothing music can evoke positive memories, reduce stress, and enhance a person's overall sense of comfort. Music can also facilitate meaningful conversations and connections between the individual nearing the end of life and their loved ones by allowing them to create moments of shared joy and reflection.

Techniques and Rituals for Supporting the End-of-Life Transition

Ceremonies and rituals have their roots in religious and cultural traditions and can provide a great deal of consolation and purpose toward the end of life. Although these rituals can take many forms, they frequently involve aspects like prayer, meditation, candle lighting, and sharing memories and experiences.

Rituals give people and their families a feeling of familiarity and structure while they deal with the psychological and spiritual challenges of death. Additionally, they can strengthen ties and a feeling of community by uniting people in support of and reverence for the person nearing the end of life.

For instance, the customary Hindu ceremony known as "Ekoddisha" offers a great deal of consolation to someone nearing death. Family members assemble around the deceased in this custom, exchanging recollections and anecdotes while praying for a calm passing. Similar to this, the Native American smudging ceremony involves burning sacred herbs to purify and cleanse the body and spirit, fostering serenity and peace. For another instance, the Jewish "Vigil of the Dead" creates a sense of community and support by bringing friends and family together to pray and console individuals nearing the end of their lives.

These customs not only offer solace to the terminally ill individual but also offer their loved ones a feeling of closure and healing. They can be customized to fit certain tastes and cultural backgrounds, which adds to their significance and individuality.

For example, Rachel, who loved the outdoors, had her family gather around her hospital bed to release balloons into the sky, signifying her departure from this world and her entry into the next. Such unique and imaginative rituals can have a profoundly positive and calming effect on the lives of persons who are nearing the end, as well as their loved ones.

The making of a legacy project or memory book is another example of a meaningful ritual. This entails compiling letters, pictures, and other keepsakes that are representative of the person's relationships and life.

This activity allows the person reaching the end of their life to experience a sense of success and purpose and leave a concrete legacy for their loved ones. It also provides a chance for introspection and the commemoration of a life well lived, resulting in a memorial that family and friends will treasure for a long time.

Initiating a legacy project can be a healing and uplifting experience for someone facing the end of their life. It enables people to give their loved ones advice and life lessons, ponder over their achievements, and treasure happy memories. Family, friends, and even caregivers can also participate in making the memory book. Joining together to commemorate the person's life can create a feeling of community and connection.

Emma, for example, was a gifted artist who made a lovely scrapbook with her sketches, paintings, and motivational sayings. Her friends and family helped create a beautiful homage to her life and legacy by sharing their favorite memories and writing meaningful letters to be included.

Michael took a different approach to his legacy by making a number of video messages for his grandchildren, telling them about his early years and imparting his knowledge and love. His family now treasures these passionate words as a priceless memento that will console and mentor future generations. Those who are approaching the end of their lives can ensure that their memory endures long after they pass away by involving their loved ones in such significant ceremonies.

Supporting individuals through the dying process doesn't always need to involve a ceremony or activity. The presence of loved ones and friends during the final days can provide immense comfort and reassurance, alleviating feelings of isolation and fear. Simple physical acts, such as holding hands or gentle massage, can convey love and support in a powerful and immediate way. Open and honest conversations about feelings and memories can also provide comfort as bonds are strengthened, and both the individual nearing the end of life and their loved ones can gain emotional closure.

Hospice care and the presence of death doulas can also improve the end-of-life experience. As mentioned previously, hospice care is centered on palliative care, which includes emotional and spiritual assistance in addition to managing medical symptoms to provide physical relief and comfort. Death doulas supplement this care by providing a consistent, empathetic presence and tailored assistance, attending to the specific needs and desires of the person reaching the end of life. When combined, these services offer a thorough strategy that respects the all-encompassing character of end-of-life care.

As you consider the journey toward the final days, it is important to recognize that each person's experience is unique. There is no one-size-fits-all approach, and the needs and desires of each person must be respected and honored. By understanding the physical, emotional, and spiritual dimensions of dying, you can provide meaningful and compassionate support that helps you and your family navigate this difficult transition with dignity and grace.

It is critical to treat each person's end-of-life journey with compassion and adaptability. For example, some end-of-life individuals choose to spend their last moments with their loved ones in the comfort of their own homes, while others would rather be in a calm, quiet setting, like a hospice or palliative care facility. Recognizing and honoring these unique preferences allows for a customized support system that prioritizes the comfort, dignity, and well-being of the person nearing the end of life.

Furthermore, culturally sensitive care that respects the values and traditions of individuals facing the end of life and integrates their religious and cultural beliefs can provide immense comfort. For instance, Sophia was a devoted Buddhist who desired that spiritual rites and readings of holy scriptures be carried out in her last days.

As she transitioned, her caregivers made sure that her desires were honored, giving her comfort and peace of mind. Valuing the individuality of every person's experience allows for a more compassionate atmosphere that recognizes the subtleties and complexities of the end-of-life journey.

Mortality is ultimately a natural and inevitable part of life. When you acknowledge this, you can face death with acceptance and calm rather than avoidance and fear. This acceptance, along with comprehensive assistance that addresses the full spectrum of physical, emotional, and spiritual needs, ensures that the final days of life are spent in the maximum degree of comfort, significance, and connection.

The end-of-life process is a journey that is full of events and challenges. Thorough and empathetic care attends to the physical changes, emotional demands, and spiritual inquiries that surface during this time.

Skilled professionals like death doulas and hospice care providers, as well as loved ones, facilitate a meaningful and dignified end-of-life experience by attending to these needs and incorporating techniques and rituals that cater to the individual's beliefs. These initiatives respect the profound and holy essence of the dying process, assisting individuals and their families in finding peace and solace as they navigate this final journey. Throughout this chapter, we've seen the importance of communication and connection. The next chapter, *Chapter 5: Communication and Connection*, will help you understand how to communicate during end-of-life care successfully.

Self-Reflective Questions

1. As a companion on this sacred journey, how can I offer true and meaningful support while navigating the inevitable problems and emotions that arise, all the while embracing the underlying beauty and deep teachings found in the journey of end-of-life?

2. How can I foster a sense of comfort, security, and peace for individuals during their end-of-life journey, and what role can I play in helping them let go of fear and anxiety surrounding death?

_____
_____
_____
_____
_____
_____
_____
_____
_____
_____
_____
_____
_____
_____
_____
_____
_____
_____
_____

3. In what ways can I support individuals in reconciling unfinished business, resolving conflicts, and finding closure with loved ones before the end of life, and how can I facilitate these important conversations?

_____
_____
_____
_____
_____
_____
_____
_____

_____
_____
_____
_____
_____
_____
_____
_____
_____
_____
_____
_____
_____

4. How can I help individuals nearing the end of life find meaning, purpose, and significance in their remaining time, and what strategies can I use to promote a sense of legacy and impact?

_____
_____
_____
_____
_____
_____
_____
_____
_____
_____
_____
_____
_____
_____
_____
_____
_____

5. What can I do to create a sacred and peaceful environment during the end-of-life transition, and how can I ensure that the individual's autonomy, dignity, and personal preferences are respected until the very end of life?

_____
_____
_____
_____
_____
_____
_____
_____
_____
_____
_____
_____
_____
_____
_____
_____
_____
_____
_____
_____
_____

Chapter 5:

Communication and Connection

Compassionate end-of-life care is centered on effective communication. Deep interactions are required to genuinely comprehend and address the concerns of those approaching their life's end. Along with gaining useful knowledge, these exchanges offer emotional and spiritual support, easing anxieties and promoting a stronger sense of connection. Active listening, empathy, and compassionate presence can facilitate conversations that respect the dying person's desires and legacy, making them feel heard, respected, and loved.

Navigating delicate and emotionally charged interactions is a critical component of good communication in end-of-life care. Examining intricate subjects like pain management, bereavement support, and advance care planning can be sensitive but necessary. By approaching these conversations with compassion, tolerance, and understanding, it is possible to make someone facing the end of life feel more at ease and capable of making decisions about their care.

Active Listening, Empathy, and Compassionate Presence

Active listening is one of the most crucial communication skills in end-of-life care. It entails being fully present with the individual in front of you by putting aside your own ideas and concerns, giving them your whole attention, comprehending what they're saying, giving a considered response, and keeping in mind what they stated. By listening actively, you can fully appreciate what the individual is saying and empathize with them, letting them know that their words and feelings matter. Being genuinely heard during such a vulnerable time may be immensely reassuring. Active listening extends beyond verbal communication. As people get closer to the end of life, they may not be able to speak and instead use nonverbal cues like touch to communicate. Individuals may become completely unresponsive in the last days or hours of life. While they may not be able to respond, hearing is often the last sense to go, so it is crucial to keep talking to them in a reassuring, caring manner to remind them of your presence and try to bring them as much calm as you can.

Empathy is a vital aspect of end-of-life communication. It is the capacity to feel another person's pain, place oneself in their position, and comprehend their emotional state. However, empathy is not the same as pity, which is just feeling bad for someone. Empathy provides genuine emotional support and enables a higher level of connection. Establishing this connection can be achieved by nonverbal clues like keeping eye contact, nodding, and, when appropriate, gently touching them, as well as verbal affirmations such as confirming their experiences and acknowledging their feelings.

Reducing feelings of loneliness and isolation is one of the biggest advantages of empathy in end-of-life care. People approaching the end of life are more willing to open up and divulge their deepest worries and fears when they feel heard and understood, which often results in a deeper connection that is immensely comforting in a period of extreme uncertainty. For instance, following his diagnosis, Dwayne, a 65-year-old man nearing the end of his life, felt incredibly isolated and alone. But as his caregiver, Maria, listened to his worries and showed empathy for how he was feeling, he started to open up and talk about his fears and anxieties. Dwayne felt much better because of this connection, which made him feel less alone and more understood, ultimately improving his general well-being.

Empathy can also help to reduce anxiety and stress in those facing end-of-life. When individuals feel heard and validated, they are more likely to feel calm and at peace. This can be especially important during a time when medical interventions and treatment options can be overwhelming. By taking the time to listen and empathize, caregivers can help alleviate some of the burden and uncertainty that comes with a terminal diagnosis.

For instance, Rachel, a hospice patient, was struggling to come to terms with her diagnosis and was feeling overwhelmed by the number of medical options available to her. Her caregiver, John, took the time to listen to her concerns and empathize with her fears, helping her to feel more calm and centered. This empathy helped Rachel to make informed decisions about her care and to feel more in control of her situation.

Furthermore, empathy can help to promote a sense of dignity and respect in those facing end-of-life. When individuals feel heard and valued, they are more likely to feel dignified and respected. This is particularly crucial as individuals may be feeling vulnerable and powerless. By taking the time to listen and empathize, caregivers can help to promote a sense of dignity and respect, which can greatly improve the quality of life of those facing their last days. For example, Michael, a 70-year-old man facing the end of his life, felt deeply disrespected and undervalued by his medical team. However, when his caregiver, Sarah, took the time to listen to his concerns and empathize with his feelings, he began to feel more dignified and respected. This empathy helped Michael to feel more confident and in control of his situation, greatly improving his overall well-being.

To sum up, empathy is a critical component of end-of-life care. Caretakers can facilitate a greater sense of connection and understanding, lessen feelings of loneliness and isolation, reduce stress and worry, and uphold the dignity and respect of persons facing the end of their lives by taking the time to listen and empathize with them. In doing this, we can support individuals nearing the end of their lives and make them feel more comfortable and supported at this trying time.

Meaningful Conversations About Death, Wishes, and Legacy

End-of-life care also includes facilitating meaningful conversations about dying, wishes, and legacy. Although these conversations might be challenging, they're essential for ensuring that the person's preferences are recognized and honored. The first step in facilitating meaningful conversations is establishing an open, safe, and comfortable setting that encourages the free expression of thoughts and feelings. Next, use open-ended questions to encourage people to communicate their experiences, concerns, and desires. For instance, you may ask, "What are some things that are important to you right now?" or "How are you feeling about everything that's happening?"

It's also essential to explore the individual's values, beliefs, and goals for their remaining time. This can involve discussing their fears, hopes, and dreams, as well as their preferences for pain management, life-sustaining treatments, and other aspects of their care. By engaging in these conversations, you can help those facing end-of-life clarify their priorities and make informed decisions about their care.

Take, for example, a social worker, Michelle, who sat down with the person she was caring for, David, to discuss his wishes for his final days. Through a series of open and honest conversations, Michelle helped David articulate his desire to spend quality time with his family, listen to his favorite music, and enjoy his beloved hobbies. By honoring these wishes, Michelle ensured that David's remaining time was filled with joy, love, and connection. Their story demonstrates the importance of open communication and empathy in creating a supportive environment that acknowledges the complexities and nuances of the dying process.

Supporting people in expressing their desires for their legacy and care at the end of their lives can be immensely powerful. It can involve discussing advance directives, hospice care, and medical intervention preferences, as well as their wishes for their legacy and how they want to be remembered. By allowing individuals nearing the end of their lives to feel more in charge of their last days and making sure that their loved ones are informed of their wishes, these conversations can help people feel at peace and find closure.

Making a legacy project is one way to organize discussions about how the person nearing the end of life wants to be remembered. Legacy projects can involve writing letters, making art, or making movies for loved ones so the individual can share their knowledge, experiences, and life lessons. For her project, 75-year-old Rachel, who was nearing the end of her life, wrote a number of letters to her grandkids in which she discussed her childhood, her morals, and her aspirations for their futures. Writing these letters, which her grandkids will cherish for years to come, gave Rachel a sense of fulfillment and purpose as they ensured her wisdom would live on in her family.

Michael took a different approach to his legacy project. He recorded a video for his loved ones expressing his appreciation, love, and encouragement. Through this legacy initiative, he was able to give his family and friends consolation and direction, leaving a lasting reminder of his love and knowledge. Rachel and Michael's examples show that legacy projects can assist those nearing the end of their lives in finding meaning, purpose, and tranquility by encouraging them to communicate their desires and leave a legacy.

Sharing memories and stories can also be a powerful way to connect with and honor the individual's life. Talking about favorite memories, significant life events, and the people who have meant the most to them not only provides comfort and joy but also helps to create a rich tapestry of their life that can be cherished by their loved ones long after they are gone. It can also help those facing end-of-life to feel valued and remembered by reinforcing the significance of their life and legacy.

Asking open-ended questions while listening to their story can elicit further details about their experiences and emotions, leading to thought-provoking discussions that foster deeper empathy and understanding. For example, you might inquire, "What was your favorite childhood vacation?" or "How did you meet your spouse?", for example. These questions can reveal undiscovered aspects of their life narrative and offer a more profound comprehension of their principles, interests, and objectives.

Also, consider taking notes during these discussions or recording them in a scrapbook or journal. This can leave a legacy of their recollections and stories that their loved ones will be able to cherish for a very long time. To sum up, connecting with others and communicating are essential to delivering compassionate end-of-life care. A crucial element of this care is facilitating meaningful discussions that respect the desires and legacies of those nearing the end of life through active listening, empathy, and compassionate presence. These exchanges give people the vital emotional and spiritual support they need to face death with dignity and grace, as well as assist their loved ones. Excellent communication builds the bridge of understanding and comfort required to make sure that everyone feels heard, respected, and loved during this significant adjustment. Death doulas can help guide individuals facing the end of life, their loved ones, and anyone else involved in this journey. So, in the next chapter, we'll take a closer look at the essential qualities of a death doula.

Self-Reflective Questions

1. How can I build genuine connections with people and their families via deep listening, empathy, and genuine presence?

_____
_____
_____
_____
_____
_____
_____
_____
_____
_____
_____
_____
_____
_____
_____
_____
_____
_____

2. How can I create a safe and empathetic space for individuals to express their fears, worries, and concerns about their end-of-life journey, and what active listening skills can I develop to validate their emotions?

_____
_____
_____
_____
_____
_____
_____
_____
_____
_____
_____
_____
_____
_____
_____
_____
_____
_____
_____
_____

3. What communication strategies can I use to ensure that the individual's unique needs, values, and goals are respected and honored during the end-of-life transition, and how can I involve their loved ones in the conversation?

_____
_____
_____
_____
_____
_____
_____

_____

_____

_____

_____

_____

_____

_____

_____

_____

_____

_____

_____

4. In what ways can I facilitate open and honest conversations about death and dying, and how can I help individuals and their loved ones navigate the emotional and psychological complexities of the end-of-life journey?

_____

_____

_____

_____

_____

_____

_____

_____

_____

_____

_____

_____

_____

_____

_____

_____

5. How can I maintain emotional intimacy and connection with individuals and their loved ones during the end-of-life transition, even in the midst of physical decline and increasing dependence on others for care?

_____
_____
_____
_____
_____
_____
_____
_____
_____
_____
_____
_____
_____
_____
_____
_____
_____
_____
_____
_____
_____

Chapter 6:

Practical Considerations for Death

Doulas

Among the many practical tasks a death doula does are those that ensure your family members or loved ones receive the care and support they need on their final journey. Developing a personalized end-of-life care plan that considers the unique needs, preferences, and values of the person nearing the end of life and their family is one of the most crucial tasks. Comprehensive discussions with the individual and their loved ones are necessary to determine the individual preferences for medical care, comfort measures, and emotional and spiritual support.

To start putting together a successful care plan, death doulas first confer with the person who will be under their care and their family members. Ideally, these talks should cover a wide variety of end-of-life care-related subjects, including pain control, preferred care settings (such as a hospital, hospice, or at home), and specific wishes for the last phases of life and after death. Death doulas prompt their clients to communicate their expectations, concerns, and hopes to ensure that the care plan takes these into account. This agreement ensures that the individual's desires are honored and respected and is available for all parties to use as a guide.

It is important that death doulas address not just the medical and comfort needs of individuals approaching the end of their life but also their emotional and spiritual needs. In addition to finding emotional support systems like friends, family, or spiritual mentors, this may involve finding a way to incorporate their beliefs and values and addressing their worries. A death doula might, for example, support a profoundly spiritual client who wants to ensure that their final moments are lived in line with their religious beliefs.

A visit by spiritual leaders or the scheduling of certain rites or rituals could be part of the care plan. Preparing the client's loved ones for possible challenges is an essential part of end-of-life care planning. In addition to providing them with information and support to help them cope with the loss of a loved one, this may involve having a conversation with them about their aspirations, concerns, and expectations. For instance, a death doula could provide emotional support during trying times or teach family members how to manage a loved one's symptoms.

A death doula can also help discuss legacy projects with individuals approaching the end of their life. These projects provide a sense of direction and closure and allow them to leave a lasting legacy. This could involve recording anecdotes, writing letters to family members, or maintaining a memory journal. These projects can be a powerful means of providing comfort to surviving family members and honoring the life and legacy of the deceased who was under their care.

Ensuring that those nearing the end of their life receive the support and care they need to die comfortably and with dignity is the ultimate goal of a customized end-of-life care plan. A death doula can help ensure that the care plan honors the client's beliefs and interests by having open conversations and documenting the client's wishes. The aim is to create a holistic plan that provides comfort, consolation, and closure for individuals approaching the end of their lives and their loved ones. A death doula, for example, can assist a client who wants to die at home, surrounded by loved ones, by making the necessary arrangements for their physical and spiritual care. Above all, death doulas establish customized care plans to make sure that their client's final days are filled with love, dignity, and compassion.

Death Doulas and the Healthcare System

Another essential part of a death doula's duties is advocating on behalf of clients' preferences inside the healthcare system. The healthcare system can be confusing and intimidating for people dealing with end-of-life concerns.

Serving as a liaison between the person under their care, their family, and medical professionals, death doulas make sure that their clients' choices are understood and honored by everyone involved. This could entail helping the client converse with their healthcare team, going to medical appointments, and taking part in care meetings.

A death doula's primary role as an advocate for their clients is to guide them through the convoluted healthcare system. This could be providing clarification on treatment alternatives, elucidating medical language, or assisting in the communication between various healthcare providers. To clarify a client's intentions, a death doula may accompany them to a medical consultation and assist with inquiries regarding treatment options. Alternatively, they may arrange for a call with a healthcare professional.

A crucial component of advocacy is making sure the autonomy of the person reaching the end of life is maintained throughout the dying process. Often, this means helping them make difficult decisions about their care, such as continuing with intense therapy or choosing palliative care. By offering emotional support and practical direction throughout the dying process, death doulas can help people nearing the end of life feel strong and in charge of their care.

A death doula may also act as an advocate for the client's family and friends, guiding them through their own emotions and anxieties as well as assisting them in understanding the wishes of the person nearing the end of life. This could entail helping the client and their loved ones have discussions about their desires and preferences or offering education and assistance regarding end-of-life care. A death doula could, for instance, facilitate a discussion regarding the client's wishes for pain treatment with their family or assist them in understanding the significance of honoring their wish to pass away at home.

Ultimately, advocacy is about ensuring that the client's values and interests are respected during the dying process. A death doula provides emotional support, advocacy, and guidance to help clients and their loved ones feel more empowered and guarantee that their wishes are met. A death doula can, for example, help a client who wants to die at home surrounded by family members by making the necessary arrangements to make that happen.

Ultimately, death doulas are vital for defending the choices of those under their care, ensuring that they get love, respect, and kindness in their final moments.

Effective advocacy requires a broad understanding of the healthcare system, including options for end-of-life care, advance healthcare directives, and patient rights. Every message sent to and from healthcare professionals needs to be documented, and following up in writing with medical providers is always a good idea. Additionally, information about end-of-life decision-making and its legal implications, as well as hospice and palliative care, should be easily accessible. Given this information, death doulas can empower those under their care to make choices that align with their values and tastes.

Integrating practical tools like notebooks and templates is crucial for successful death doulas. There are templates for daily care schedules, pain management records, and advance care plans to assist, organize, and make sense of the various components of end-of-life care. These tools provide organization and ensure that important information is not overlooked. Many states, territories, and countries have different laws and rules surrounding end-of-life. It's crucial that death doulas understand and follow the laws pertaining to wills, advance care directives, and other documents in the area they practice.

Journaling as a Therapeutic Technique

For clients and their families, journaling can be an effective therapeutic tool during the end-of-life journey as it offers a creative and secure outlet for expression and reflection. It is suggested that individuals nearing the end of life keep diaries so they can process their thoughts, emotions, and reflections in a way that is both empowering and cathartic. This practice can be emotionally consoling as it assists individuals in processing challenging emotions and allows them to create a meaningful record of their experiences. Those approaching the end of their lives may find journaling to be an extremely useful tool. It can help people accept and come to terms with their mortality and discover meaning and purpose for the time they have left.

Writing down their hopes, fears, and reflections can help them gain a better understanding of who they are and what has happened to them, as well as begin the process of coming to terms with and accepting their past. For example, someone nearing the end of life may write about their gratitude for the time they have spent with loved ones or about their concerns about the future.

Journaling can prove to be a very helpful resource for family members who are struggling to manage the emotional burden of grief and providing care for others. Any family member or close friend can pen down their fondest memories of their loved one or express their concerns about how they will cope with their grief.

By keeping a journal, they can process their own feelings, memories, and reflections as well as better understand the experience of their loved one, providing them a sense of continuity and connection even in the face of accepting the death of a loved one.

In addition to reducing emotional suffering and promoting reflection, journaling can serve as an important record of the journey toward death. In addition to finding comfort in the memories and lessons learned, those facing the end of life and their families can honor and recall their prior experiences by going over their journals. For example, a client may write about their most treasured moments of happiness and beauty or their biggest insights.

Death doulas can offer guidance and support for journaling by supplying necessary resources and advice. Additionally, death doulas should consider keeping a journey themselves as a way to reflect on their own emotions and experiences. Doing this can provide a better understanding of the end-of-life experience and allow death doulas to be better equipped to support and care for their clients.

Journaling can help those nearing the end of life, their families, and even death doulas better understand and cope with the wide range of emotions and experiences related to the dying process. By endorsing and encouraging this practice, death doulas can assist their clients in leaving a lasting legacy of love and wisdom, as well as give them comfort, meaning, and purpose in their final days.

In summary, being a death doula involves several distinct and important practical components. By creating individualized care plans, advocating on their behalf within the healthcare system, and providing them with access to additional support services, death doulas ensure that those under their care receive comprehensive and compassionate treatment. Utilizing helpful tools like diaries and templates increases their ability to support clients and their families as they approach death. It is the duty of a death doula to provide people with all-encompassing care that honors their unique needs and choices, supporting them and their loved ones with dignity and grace at this profoundly transformative time. It is also important for death doulas and caregivers to take care of themselves. Therefore, the following chapter will focus on self-care.

Self-Reflective Questions

1. A few examples of the practical responsibilities and logistical issues related to end-of-life care are ensuring a dignified and peaceful dying, setting up resources, and providing comfort measures. How can I continue providing the emotional and spiritual support that is essential to the function of a death doula?

_____

_____

_____

_____

_____

_____

_____

_____

_____

_____

_____

_____

_____

_____

_____

_____

_____

_____

_____

_____

_____

_____

2. What steps can I take to ensure that the individual's advance care directive and other legal documents are respected and enforced, even when they may no longer be able to communicate their wishes?

_____

_____

_____

_____

_____

_____

_____

_____

_____

_____

_____

_____

_____

_____

_____

_____

_____

_____

3. How can I facilitate effective communication and coordination among the individual's healthcare providers, caregivers, and loved ones to ensure seamless and comprehensive care during the end-of-life transition?

_____

_____

_____

_____

_____

_____

_____

_____

_____

_____

_____

_____

_____

_____

_____

_____

_____

_____

_____

_____

4. What practical strategies can I employ to help individuals and their families navigate the complexities of medical decision-making, pain management, and symptom control during the end-of-life journey?

_____

_____

_____

_____

_____

_____

_____

_____

_____

_____

_____

_____

_____

_____

_____

_____

_____

_____

_____

5. In what ways can I provide emotional and spiritual support to the individual and their loved ones during the dying process while also acknowledging and respecting their unique cultural, religious, or secular beliefs and traditions?

_____

_____

_____

_____

_____

_____

_____

_____

_____

_____

_____

_____

_____

_____

_____

Chapter 7:

Self-Care for Death Doulas

and Caregivers

Caring for individuals at the end of life is immensely rewarding but can be an emotionally taxing role. Death doulas and caregivers bear witness to profound moments of transition, deep grief, and significant loss. The emotional toll of this work can be heavy, making it essential to prioritize self-care to manage compassion fatigue and prevent burnout.

Feelings of emotional numbness, detachment, and hopelessness might be signs of compassion fatigue, a syndrome brought on by extended exposure to pain and trauma. Physical symptoms, including weariness, headaches, and sleep difficulties, might also result from it. Compassion fatigue can impair your capacity to deliver compassionate care, resulting in emotional exhaustion and burnout if left unchecked.

Consequently, it is essential to establish self-care practices in order to preserve mental and physical health. This is a must rather than a luxury if you want to make sure you can keep providing those nearing the end of life and their families the care and assistance they require.

Strategies for Managing Compassion Fatigue and Burnout

Prioritizing self-compassion is one way to counter compassion fatigue and burnout. Rather than attempting to repress or ignore feelings, self-compassion entails acknowledging and accepting feelings so that you can address the emotional toll of caring for someone at the end of life. For instance, you may plan frequent pauses, do deep breathing exercises or meditation, or ask fellow caregivers or a therapist for help.

Another crucial tactic is setting limits or boundaries. This might be difficult, especially if you have a strong feeling of duty to those under your care and are really committed to the work. However, boundaries are crucial for preserving mental and physical well-being. Setting clear boundaries for your time, energy, and emotional resources can help avoid burnout and increase your capacity to offer compassionate care.

Developing a network of friends, family, and fellow caregivers who can offer emotional support and connection is also crucial. This can be especially useful when confronted with difficult circumstances or during emergencies. Having a support system allows you to talk to others who understand the demands of caring for someone nearing the end of life about your feelings and worries, and you can also receive advice and assistance.

Finally, it's important to pursue hobbies and pursuits that make you happy and fulfilled away from caregiving. Engaging in activities like hobbies or spending quality time with your friends and family can help you refuel your physical and emotional vitality and keep your sense of fulfillment and purpose.

Being a caregiver for those facing the end of life is an extremely fulfilling but emotionally demanding job. Setting boundaries, practicing self-compassion, prioritizing self-care, building a support system, and partaking in joyful and fulfilling activities are all crucial to preserving your capacity to offer compassionate assistance. By employing these tactics, you can avoid burnout, deal with compassionate fatigue, and maintain your physical and mental well-being.

The Importance of Self-Care for Death Doulas

Those who provide end-of-life care frequently experience burnout and compassion fatigue. Often referred to as the "cost of caring," compassion fatigue is the result of being overly sensitive to and concerned about others all the time. Burnout, which is a condition of extreme physical, emotional, and mental exhaustion, is a related condition and can result from excessive workloads and ongoing stress. Identifying the symptoms of these conditions, such as feelings of helplessness, anger, persistent exhaustion, and a lowered sense of personal achievement, is the first step toward treating them.

To manage compassion fatigue and burnout, it is crucial to implement regular self-care practices. These practices might include physical activities like yoga, walking, or dancing, which help to release stress and improve overall well-being. Mindfulness and meditation can also be powerful tools to ground yourself in the present moment and reduce anxiety. Setting boundaries is equally important; learn to say no when necessary and ensure you have adequate time to rest and recharge between caregiving responsibilities.

It's critical to understand the value of looking out for oneself as a caregiver. Prioritizing your needs over others may make you feel selfish, but the truth is that you cannot pour from an empty cup. If you want to genuinely support those who are nearing the end of their lives, you must look after yourself. This may mean going for a 30-minute stroll outside during your lunch break, centering yourself with yoga in the morning, or scheduling a soothing bath once a week. Whatever it is, give it top attention.

Overcommitting is a typical mistake many caretakers make. Despite believing you can manage everything, you can't, and you shouldn't have to. It's critical to acknowledge your boundaries. When a request seems too big or unachievable, learn to say no. Recall that accepting yourself first implies saying no to requests from other people.

Asking for help from others is an important part of self-care. You don't need to face this alone, so seek assistance from friends, family, or fellow caregivers who are aware of the responsibilities involved in providing end-of-life care. If you don't have these people nearby, you can connect with people who have similar experiences by joining an online community or support group. These relationships can be a lifeline, offering comfort and approval when you need it most.

It's also crucial to take pauses to give yourself time to relax, rejuvenate, and escape the heavy emotional toll caregiving can take. These pauses may be vacations or just taking a few days off from caring for others. Whatever it is, it must feed your body, mind, and spirit. As you negotiate the challenging emotions and responsibilities of providing end-of-life care, keep in mind that you are not alone. Many have gone through this experience before you and followed the journey to the end. Rest assured that you are a member of a wider community dedicated to providing compassionate care as well as self-care. Ultimately, keep in mind that caring for yourself is necessary, not selfish. Making time for your own health will enable you to be there for those who are nearing the end of their lives and provide them with the support, empathy, and care they require on their final journey. Take a deep breath, put on your own oxygen mask, and keep in mind that taking care of yourself is essential—self-care is not a luxury.

Developing Resilience as a Death Doula

Resilience is the capacity to adjust and recover from adversity. Cultivating resilience in the context of end-of-life care entails learning coping mechanisms for the persistent presence of loss and grief. One useful tactic is processing your experiences and feelings through introspective activities like writing. Writing down your ideas and emotions gives you a way to communicate your grief and might help you comprehend your journey more fully.

Another great way to develop resilience is through building a support system. As previously mentioned, building a support network is essential for your well-being as a death doula or caregiver, but it can also help develop resilience. Connecting with others who understand the unique challenges and rewards of caring for those at the end of life can provide a sense of camaraderie and reduce feelings of isolation. Sharing experiences, advice, and support with peers can be a powerful way to navigate the complex emotional landscape of end-of-life care, building resilience along the way.

Connecting with other death doulas and caregivers through professional organizations is one approach to creating a support system. These communities can offer a secure setting where you can talk about your experiences, ask questions, and get advice from people who have been through similar experiences. Joining a national death doula association or local hospice organization can help you connect with people who share your passion for end-of-life care. Another great tool for creating a support system is joining an online community.

You can ask questions, share your experiences, and get advice from others on blogs, online forums, and social media groups. Individuals who work in rural or isolated places, where networking opportunities may be scarce, may find these networks particularly beneficial.

Connecting with peers and coworkers in your community is just as vital for developing resilience as participating in online forums and professional groups. In-person events, like conferences, workshops, and training sessions, can help you meet people as passionate about end-of-life care as you are. These gatherings can foster a sense of community and connection, crucial for resilience, while also offering chances for learning, growth, and networking.

You can take care of yourself and give the greatest care possible to individuals nearing the end of their lives by developing resilience. Processing your emotions and experiences through introspective activities, like writing or connecting with others through building a support system, can help you cope with the emotional challenges that come with providing end-of-life care.

Accessing Resources for Professional and Personal Growth

Accessing resources for personal and professional growth is another critical component of self-care for death doulas and caregivers. While engaging in education and training opportunities is an excellent way to access these resources, connecting with others who are aware of the special difficulties and benefits associated with providing end-of-life care can provide a wealth of knowledge and support that will enable you to give people facing the end of life the finest care possible.

For instance, a colleague with expertise in caring for people with a particular kind of terminal illness may have insightful counsel and recommendations on providing the best care under those specific circumstances.

Alternatively, a peer who has worked extensively with those experiencing difficult emotional or spiritual problems could have invaluable advice on providing comfort during those difficult times.

Attending education and training events, such as workshops, seminars, and conferences, provides access to the most up-to-date resources for professional and personal growth, providing you with the tools and insights you need to stay current and confident in your work. These events are also opportunities to build your professional network and learn from other caregivers by exchanging best practices and learning from diverse experiences. For example, you may go to a workshop on advance care planning and learn about the most recent medical and legal advancements in end-of-life care. Alternatively, at a conference on grief counseling, you could hear about best practices from professionals who specialize in that field.

Aside from imparting knowledge on end-of-life subjects, these gatherings also offer opportunities to contemplate your personal behaviors and principles. You may, for instance, go to a session on compassionate listening to learn more about the value of empathy and attentive listening when caring for the dying. Taking these opportunities can help you recharge, refocus, and return to caregiving with a fresh sense of purpose and enthusiasm. It's crucial to understand that providing care requires not only expertise and knowledge but also emotional fortitude and personal development. Accessing resources for professional and personal growth can provide you the opportunity to examine your own spiritual and emotional needs and build the self-awareness and self-care techniques necessary for long-term caregiving. One way to learn about the significance of attending to your own emotional and spiritual needs is to participate in a course on mindfulness and self-compassion. Alternatively, you may go to a retreat designed just for caretakers, where you can take a break from your everyday obligations and concentrate on your own personal development and rejuvenation.

Ultimately, providing individuals nearing the end of life the best care possible requires having access to tools for professional and personal growth. As a caregiver, you can make sure that you are always giving the best care possible while adhering to your values and passions by continuing to learn, grow, and develop. Remember, providing care is an undertaking, not a final goal. Therefore, continuous work, devotion, and commitment are necessary. Gaining access to tools for both professional and personal development will help you stay motivated, energized, and dedicated to caring for those nearing the end of their lives.

Seeking Support From a Therapist or Supervisor

Providing end-of-life care is a challenging but rewarding vocation, and professional supervision or counseling can be invaluable for processing the emotional complexities of caregiving. Speaking with a therapist or supervisor who specializes in end-of-life care can provide a safe space to explore your feelings and develop coping strategies. These professionals can offer guidance on managing the emotional toll of caregiving and help you navigate the challenging situations that arise when looking after someone nearing the end of life. For instance, you might find it difficult to move on after losing someone under your care who was very dear to you. A therapist or supervisor can offer an impartial and secure environment in which to process this loss, explore your emotions, and create coping mechanisms. They might also provide advice on how to keep a professional distance while still showing sympathy. Therapists and supervisors can also assist with creating coping mechanisms for the emotional demands of end-of-life caregiving. These coping mechanisms typically involve self-care methods like deep breathing exercises or meditation, as well as strategies for setting clear boundaries and prioritizing your needs.

It's also critical to acknowledge that providing end-of-life care can be a very solitary occupation, and asking for help from those aware of the difficulties and rewards of this vocation can be quite helpful. Therapists, supervisors, or simply other caregivers can make you feel less alone and more supported by offering a sense of community and connection. Additionally, therapists or supervisors can assist with the cultivation of a development mindset, which is necessary for professional caregivers who want to advance in their position. Through self-evaluation and identification of areas of strength and weakness, you can create professional and personal growth strategies that will keep you inspired and involved in your work. Being a caretaker requires seeking expert counseling or supervision to work through personal feelings, create coping mechanisms, and handle the emotional demands of your job. Providing the best possible care for people nearing the end of life while also taking care of yourself is possible with the support of a therapist or supervisor.

In conclusion, self-care is essential for death doulas and caregivers to sustain their ability to provide compassionate and effective end-of-life care. By recognizing the signs of compassion fatigue and burnout, implementing regular self-care practices, and cultivating resilience, caregivers can navigate the emotional challenges of this work. Building a support network and accessing resources for personal and professional growth further enhances the capacity to care for others. Remember that personal well-being is crucial to providing quality care; by nurturing yourself, you ensure that you can continue to offer the empathy, support, and presence that are so vital to those nearing the end of life. So far, we've discussed the vital but challenging role death doulas play in the end-of-life journey. The next chapter will take you through the training and certification process for a death doula.

Self-Reflective Questions

1. How can I prioritize my own well-being, set boundaries, and practice self-care in a way that sustains me emotionally, physically, and spiritually as a death doula or caregiver, enabling me to continue offering compassionate support to others during times of loss and transition?

2. What self-care practices can I commit to on a regular basis, such as meditation, exercise, or creative pursuits, to maintain my emotional resilience and prevent compassion fatigue?

_____
_____
_____
_____
_____
_____
_____
_____
_____
_____
_____
_____
_____
_____
_____
_____
_____
_____
_____
_____
_____

3. How can I establish and maintain healthy boundaries with my clients and their loved ones to ensure that I am not overextending myself emotionally or physically?

_____
_____
_____
_____
_____
_____
_____
_____

_____
_____
_____
_____
_____
_____
_____
_____
_____
_____
_____
_____
_____

4. In what ways can I cultivate a support network of peers, mentors, or supervisors who can offer emotional support, guidance, and validation during challenging times?

_____
_____
_____
_____
_____
_____
_____
_____
_____
_____
_____
_____
_____
_____
_____
_____
_____
_____
_____
_____
_____

5. What strategies can I employ to acknowledge and process my own grief and emotional responses to the losses I witness, and how can I create a safe space for self-reflection and emotional release?

_____

_____

_____

_____

_____

_____

_____

_____

_____

_____

_____

_____

_____

_____

_____

_____

_____

_____

_____

_____

_____

_____

Chapter 8:

Becoming a Death Doula: Training and Certification

The path to becoming a death doula is both deeply personal and professionally enriching. As you consider this journey, it is essential to explore the educational pathways available to you. Workshops, courses, and certification programs offer a structured way to gain the knowledge and skills needed to support individuals and families through the end-of-life process. These educational experiences provide foundational understanding in areas such as grief counseling, pain management, spiritual care, and the legal aspects of end-of-life planning.

Apart from academic pursuits, many would-be-death doulas look for mentorship and apprenticeship programs. These can offer invaluable practical experience and the ability to learn from seasoned death doulas by shadowing them during client visits or being matched with a longer-term mentor who can provide support and guidance. Furthermore, aspiring death doulas can pursue training around ethical considerations and professional standards or even get certified, although this is not required to practice.

Educational Pathways for Aspiring Death Doulas

Educational pathways for aspiring death doulas vary widely in terms of content, duration, and depth. Some programs are brief, offering intensive weekend workshops, while others are more comprehensive, spanning several months or even years. These programs often include both theoretical and practical components, covering topics such as the physical processes of dying, emotional and psychological support, and effective communication techniques.

Community institutions, online learning environments, or organizations specializing in end-of-life care may provide courses that are flexible enough to fit your schedule and learning style. A hospice organization may, for instance, offer a certification program that combines classroom learning with practical experience in a hospice setting. If you'd rather learn at your own pace, you could choose an online course that addresses the spiritual and emotional facets of end-of-life care.

It is crucial to confirm that the program is respectable and accredited, regardless of the educational path you decide on. Several organizations have set standards for death doula education and certification to guarantee that graduates have a solid foundation in the information and abilities required to support people and families through the end-of-life journey. So, search for programs that have been approved by national associations, such as the International End-of-Life Doula Association or the National End-of-Life Doula Alliance. When choosing an educational program, it's also important to take into account the particular areas of concentration that are most significant to you.

For instance, if you are interested in working with clients who are going through complex loss, you should seek a program that offers specific training in grief counseling. Similarly, if you want to work with clients considering alternative therapies, like art or music therapy, you might want a program that provides training in these fields. A strong dedication to learning and preparation is necessary to become a death doula. You can acquire the necessary information and abilities to assist people and families during the end-of-life phase by investigating the available education options and choosing one that suits you. Whether it's a quick workshop, an intensive course, or an extensive certification program, finding a program that fits your objectives and offers the support you need is essential to ensuring you reach your aspirations.

Practical Experience and Mentorship Opportunities

In addition to formal education, gaining practical experience is crucial to developing the confidence and competence needed for being a death doula. Mentorship opportunities can be invaluable in this regard.

Working under the guidance of experienced death doulas allows you to observe and participate in end-of-life care in real-world settings. This hands-on experience helps you apply theoretical knowledge, hone your skills, and navigate the complexities of supporting individuals nearing the end of life and their families. Mentors can provide feedback, share insights from their own practice, and offer emotional support as you progress in your journey.

Practical experience can also be gained through volunteering in hospice settings, nursing homes, or community support groups. These environments expose you to the diverse needs of those facing end-of-life and their families, broadening your understanding of the different ways people experience and cope with dying. Volunteering not only builds your skills but also deepens your empathy and reinforces your commitment to providing compassionate care.

Making deep connections with people facing the end of their lives is one of the most fulfilling parts of helping in hospice settings. Spending time with these people allows you to better understand their individual needs and concerns by hearing about their experiences and sharing your own. As you watch the challenges, bravery, resiliency, and strength of those approaching the end of their lives, you may realize how incredibly touching it is to be there during their final days.

For instance, while volunteering at a hospice, you could be tasked with spending time with a person experiencing loneliness and isolation. You forge a deep bond by sitting with them, sharing in their hardships, and listening to their tales. You may begin to brighten their days with small presents, like a beloved book or a bunch of flowers. If they need help navigating the difficulties of their condition, you may volunteer to do errands or just be there for them. These acts, while simple, may take on a new meaning as you assist those on their end-of-life journey.

As you keep volunteering, you might discover that you are drawn to particular types of assistance, like legacy work or counseling for grieving. You may assist with counseling sessions for families dealing with bereavement or collaborate with a group of volunteers to make scrapbooks or memory books for patients. When you witness the difference your work is making in the lives of the people you are helping, these encounters can be quite satisfying.

Engaging in volunteer work in nursing homes can also yield significant experience, as you will be interacting with residents who may be dealing with a variety of difficulties, such as cognitive impairment or physical decline. You may just be there to be a companion and chat, or you could help with everyday tasks like feeding or cleaning. Additionally, you may collaborate with staff members to create activities and programming that meet the social and emotional needs of the residents.

Apart from helping at hospice and assisted living facilities, you might also think about volunteering in neighborhood support groups. These organizations frequently bring together people going through comparable struggles, such as caring for a loved one or losing a parent. You can encourage a sense of belonging and community among group members by conducting conversations, organizing events, or just being there to support and listen.

Another possible way to assist caregivers would be to volunteer with an organization that provides services and a temporary break for individuals taking care of loved ones. You may take the lead in talks about stress management, boundary-setting, and self-care, or you could just lend someone a sympathetic ear. Whatever option you choose, gaining mentorship and practical experience can considerably help you become a successful death doula?

Ethical Considerations and Professional Standards For Death Doulas

Ethical considerations and professional standards are fundamental to the practice of a death doula. As a death doula, you will be entrusted with intimate and sensitive aspects of people's lives, including their personal beliefs, values, and experiences. Upholding high ethical standards ensures that you provide care that is respectful, compassionate, and aligned with the wishes and needs of those facing end-of-life. One of the fundamental tenets of ethical practice for death doulas is autonomy.

This tenet implies that you respect the autonomy of individuals nearing the end of their lives to choose their own care and therapies. Respecting autonomy is especially crucial when working with clients who have complex medical issues or who must make difficult decisions regarding their care.

As an illustration, you may be assisting someone considering hospice care but is reluctant to cease intensive medical care. In this case, you may need to assist them in considering their alternatives and respect their decision-making as their death doula, even if it deviates from your own.

Dignity is also a crucial aspect of a death doula's ethical behavior. This calls for you to put the worth and dignity of those nearing the end of their lives first and to make sure they are treated with kindness and respect. When working with clients who are in pain, either physically or emotionally, or who are dealing with emotions of guilt or shame, this can be particularly crucial.

For example, a client you may be working with may need assistance with personal care or a sensitive issue like incontinence. As their death doula, you have to put their dignity first by giving them kind, considerate care and making sure they know how much they are appreciated.

A death doula's ethical practice must highlight the concept of beneficence in addition to autonomy and dignity. This implies that you have to put the health and welfare of people nearing the end of their lives first and make sure that your care and assistance are customized to meet their individual needs and circumstances.

For instance, you might be working with a client who is depressed or anxious or who is in a great deal of pain. As their death doula, you need to put their welfare first by offering techniques for managing their suffering or putting them in touch with services and support for mental health. Justice must also be given top priority in a death doula's ethical profession. It is imperative that you acknowledge the intrinsic value and merit of every person, irrespective of their origins, characteristics, or situations. This can be crucial when working with patients who have encountered discrimination, marginalization, or systemic obstacles to receiving care. For example, you may have a client who identifies as LGBTQ+ or who has encountered racism or discrimination. As their death doula, you may have to put their justice first by making sure that their particular needs and circumstances are understood and acknowledged, as well as by offering inclusive and culturally sensitive care. Professional standards and ethical considerations are essential to a death doula's work. You can provide end-of-life care that is courteous, compassionate, and in line with the needs and wishes of persons facing death by placing a high priority on autonomy, dignity, beneficence, and justice.

Professional standards for death doulas often emphasize the importance of continuous learning and self-reflection. The field of end-of-life care is constantly evolving, and staying informed about new research, techniques, and best practices is essential. Engaging in ongoing education through workshops, seminars, and professional development courses helps you stay current and maintain the highest quality of care.

Ethical practice for death doulas is not just about the care you provide for others; it's also about the care you give to yourself. Self-care is a critical aspect of ethical practice. The emotional demands of supporting dying individuals can be intense, and it is vital to ensure that you are taking care of your own mental and emotional health. Establishing boundaries, seeking supervision, and connecting with peers for support are all important strategies to prevent burnout and sustain your ability to provide empathetic care.

Certification for Death Doulas

While certification is not universally required, it can provide reassurance to clients and their families that you have met certain educational and ethical standards. Certification programs typically involve a combination of coursework, practical experience, and an evaluation of your competencies. Some organizations also require continuing education to maintain certification, ensuring that you remain up-to-date with advancements in the field.

The International End of Life Doula Association (INELDA) offers the Certified End of Life Doula (CEOLD) credential, which is one of the most well-known for death doulas. A thorough training program and at least 20 hours of supervised practical practice are prerequisites for this certification. To keep the CEOLD certification, those holding it are required to fulfill continuing education requirements every two years. The Certified Death Doula (CDD) credential, provided by the Death Doula Alliance of Canada (DDAC), is an additional alternative for certification. A minimum of 30 hours of supervised practical experience and the completion of a training program are prerequisites for this certification. Once achieved, those holding the CDD certification must fulfill continuing education requirements yearly to keep it.

In addition to general death doula certifications, certain organizations might additionally provide specific credentials in fields like grief assistance, hospice care, or palliative care. By demonstrating your proficiency in particular areas of end-of-life care, these certificates can boost your credibility with clients and their families. For example, obtaining a certification in hospice care would attest to your proficiency in offering assistance to patients undergoing hospice care. Further education and hands-on experience working with hospice patients and their families may be required for this certification.

On the other hand, a certification in bereavement support would attest to your proficiency in offering assistance to individuals who are managing mourning and loss. Additional coursework and real-world experience dealing with grieving people and families may be required for this certification. As it acknowledges your diligence and commitment to the field of end-of-life care, certification can also bring you a sense of personal and professional pleasure. Being certified validates their talents and experience, which is why many death doulas report feeling a sense of pleasure and success upon achieving them. Aside from the aforementioned certificates, certain organizations might also provide specific training courses or certifications in subjects like pain management, advanced care planning, or ethics in end-of-life care. In addition to imparting new information and abilities, these programs demonstrate your dedication to lifelong learning and career advancement. All things considered, death doulas may find great value in certification, which offers legitimacy, experience, and a feeling of both professional and personal fulfillment. Getting certified can help you advance professionally and personally, as well as reassure clients and their families that you have fulfilled ethical and educational requirements. This is true whether you decide to pursue a basic or specialized certification.

To sum up, becoming a death doula requires a dedication to ethical practice, practical experience, and education. You can ensure that you are equipped to deliver compassionate and efficient end-of-life care by enrolling in appropriate training and certification programs, obtaining practical experience through volunteer work and mentoring, and upholding strict professional standards. The benefits of this journey are immense, but it demands commitment and introspection. By providing support, comfort, and a caring presence during one of life's most difficult transitions, a death doula can have a profound impact on the lives of those who are approaching the end of their lives as well as their families. For you to fully understand the role death doulas play, the next chapter contains the insights and inspirations gained from the testimonies of seasoned death doulas.

Self-Reflective Questions

1. How can I acknowledge that genuine competence in this field stems not only from education and certification but also from a deep well of empathy, intuition, and compassion and approach my road to becoming a death doula with humility, determination, and a commitment to continuing study and personal growth?

_____

_____

_____

_____

_____

_____

_____

_____
_____
_____
_____
_____
_____
_____
_____
_____
_____
_____
_____
_____
_____

2. What specific areas of end-of-life care do I need to focus on in my training, such as grief counseling, pain management, or spiritual care, to feel confident and competent in my role as a death doula?

_____
_____
_____
_____
_____
_____
_____
_____
_____
_____
_____
_____
_____
_____
_____
_____
_____
_____
_____
_____

3. How can I ensure that my certification program or training course aligns with my personal values, beliefs, and goals as a death doula, and what criteria should I use to evaluate the quality and credibility of these programs?

_____
_____
_____
_____
_____
_____
_____
_____
_____
_____
_____
_____
_____
_____
_____
_____
_____
_____
_____
_____

4. In what ways can I continue to develop my skills and knowledge through ongoing education, networking, and professional development to stay current with best practices and emerging trends in end-of-life care?

_____
_____
_____
_____
_____
_____
_____

_____
_____
_____
_____
_____
_____
_____
_____
_____
_____
_____
_____
_____

5. What role does self-reflection and personal growth play in my development as a death doula, and how can I integrate my own experiences, values, and perspectives into my professional practice?

_____
_____
_____
_____
_____
_____
_____
_____
_____
_____
_____
_____
_____
_____
_____
_____

Chapter 9:

Insights and Inspiration

In the world of end-of-life care, the voices and experiences of seasoned death doulas offer invaluable insights and inspiration. Their journeys are marked by a deep commitment to providing compassionate care, and their stories reveal the profound impact they have on the lives of those facing end-of-life and their families. Through interviews with these dedicated professionals, you will gain a deeper understanding of the challenges they face, the triumphs they celebrate, and the wisdom they have acquired along the way.

The Journeys, Challenges, and Triumphs of Real-Life Death Doulas

One of the biggest obstacles death doulas encounter is the emotional strain of their work. As death doulas are confronted with the brutal reality of mortality daily, they must learn to cope with their own loss and emotional suffering in order to keep giving care to those who are most in need. For instance, a death doula called Clare from Georgia told me about her experience tending to a young woman who had two little children and was terminally ill with cancer. Clare remembered how she had to balance the mother and her family's needs with her own emotional reaction to the circumstance.

Death doulas gain a profound understanding of life, death, and the value of empathy and compassion in the face of suffering through their experiences. They gain an appreciation for life's fleeting nature and the significance of savoring every moment. They also grow to have a great regard for the human spirit and the amazing fortitude that people exhibit when faced with hardship.

Death doulas deal with many practical difficulties on a daily basis in addition to the psychological and spiritual aspects of their employment. They must advocate for their clients and families and find their way around the complicated healthcare system to make sure they get the help and assistance they require. Additionally, they have to manage their own time and energy in order to reconcile the demands of their jobs with their personal and professional obligations.

Many death doulas describe experiencing a profound sense of fulfillment and purpose in their job despite these difficulties. One such voice is that of Gloria, a death doula from Minnesota with over 15 years of experience. Gloria's journey began after she lost her mother to cancer. The lack of emotional support and guidance during her mother's final days left a lasting impression on her. Determined to make a difference, Gloria pursued training as a death doula. She describes her role as "a calling to bring peace and dignity to the dying process." Gloria emphasizes the importance of presence, stating, "It's not about having the right words, but about being there, fully present, offering a hand to hold and a heart to listen."

In New York, another experienced death doula, James, shares his journey of becoming a doula after retiring from a career in nursing. He explains, "I realized that while medical care is crucial, the emotional and spiritual support often gets overlooked. I wanted to fill that gap." James recounts a memorable experience with a patient named Lucy, who had no family nearby. He became her confidant, helping her create a legacy project that included letters and recorded messages for her estranged children. James reflects, "Lucy found peace knowing her words would reach her children, and I felt honored to be part of her journey."

Real-life examples like these illustrate the significant impact death doulas have on the individuals they support. Gertrude, a woman from Pennsylvania in her mid-forties, was diagnosed with a terminal illness and struggled with the fear of leaving her young children behind. Her death doula, Anne, helped her navigate these fears by facilitating open conversations with her children and helping her create memory boxes for each of them. Gertrude's husband, David, shares, "Anne's support was a lifeline. She helped us make the most of the time we had left and created lasting memories for our children."

These stories highlight the diverse ways in which death doulas provide support. Whether it's through legacy projects, emotional support, or simply being a calming presence, their impact is profound. They offer a unique blend of practical assistance and emotional nurturing, helping individuals and families find peace and meaning in the midst of loss.

Words of Wisdom From Real-Life Death Doulas

The collective wisdom of these experienced doulas underscores the essence of their work: compassion, presence, and resilience. They remind aspiring doulas that the journey is not just about supporting others but also about personal transformation. Each encounter with those facing end-of-life and their families is an opportunity to learn, grow, and deepen one's understanding of life and death.

The value of empathy and compassion in the face of pain is among the most important lessons death doulas can impart to us. Death doulas show a strong dedication to supporting people, even in the most trying and sensitive times, by traveling with those approaching the end of their lives. This compassion comes from genuinely comprehending and connecting to the experiences of others, not just from feeling sorry for them.

For instance, one death doula, Matilda from Washington, told me about her experience tending to a woman with cancer named Maria. When Maria was in pain, Matilda remembered how she would frequently grow irritated and belligerent because she was afraid of dying. Instead of avoiding her or attempting to solve her issues, Matilda listened to Maria's concerns and fears while sitting with her and holding her hand. Matilda gained Maria's trust over time, and as a result, Maria opened up to her about in innermost feelings. Maria felt more at ease as a result of Matilda's empathy and compassion, which also made it possible for them to have a deeper emotional connection.

A death doula's presence is another crucial component of her job. Those approaching the end of life need to feel seen, heard, and appreciated by those surrounding them.

This sense of presence by caring individuals can be immensely consoling, particularly during times of extreme suffering and uncertainty. Death doulas define being present as putting aside outside distractions and just being with people, expectation-free. For example, a death doula from Texas named Michael told me about his experience tending to a man named Jack, who was terminally ill with heart disease. Michael remembered how Jack had a TV obsession and would frequently become upset when his favorite shows were cut off. Instead of attempting to divert Jack's attention or persuade him to shift his focus, Michael just sat down with him and watched TV. Jack started talking more and more about his life, his regrets, and his anxieties as time went on. In Jack's last days, Michael gave him a sense of comfort and company through this small act of presence, which let them connect on a deeper level.

Death doulas also demonstrate a remarkable level of resilience in the face of adversity. Accompanying those facing end-of-life can be emotionally draining and exhausting, and death doulas must find ways to manage their own emotions and stress levels in order to continue providing care.

For those considering this path, the stories and insights shared in this chapter serve as both guidance and inspiration. The ability to provide comfort, peace, and dignity at the end of life is a profound gift, one that touches the lives of all involved.

As you contemplate becoming a death doula (or even if you are a caregiver), take these words of wisdom to heart. Understand that the journey requires dedication, empathy, and a willingness to embrace the unknown. Know that you are joining a community of compassionate individuals committed to making a difference in the world of end-of-life care. With every hand you hold and every story you hear, you will be part of a sacred journey, one that honors the essence of life itself.

In conclusion, the insights and inspiration from experienced death doulas offer a window into the profound impact of their work. Their stories of compassion, resilience, and dedication provide a roadmap for aspiring doulas, highlighting the challenges and triumphs of this unique and rewarding profession. As you embark on this journey, may you find the courage to offer your heart and presence to those nearing the end of life, and may you be inspired by the transformative power of compassionate care. The final chapter of this book will help you understand how to manage and get support through the dying process.

Self-Reflective Questions

1. How can I draw upon the insights and inspirations gleaned from the lives of experienced death doulas to deepen my own understanding of the profound nature of death and dying and to inform my practice with a greater sense of purpose, compassion, and wisdom?

_____
_____
_____
_____
_____
_____
_____
_____
_____
_____
_____
_____
_____
_____
_____
_____
_____
_____
_____
_____

2. What lessons can I learn from the experiences of seasoned death doulas, and how can I apply their wisdom to my own practice and approach to end-of-life care?

_____
_____
_____
_____
_____
_____
_____
_____
_____
_____
_____
_____
_____
_____
_____
_____
_____
_____
_____

3. In what ways can I draw inspiration from the stories of death doulas who have witnessed profound moments of transformation, healing, and closure at the end of life?

_____
_____
_____
_____
_____
_____
_____
_____

_____

_____

_____

_____

_____

_____

_____

_____

_____

_____

_____

_____

4. How can I use the insights and experiences shared by seasoned death doulas to inform my own personal growth and development as a compassionate and empathetic caregiver?

_____

_____

_____

_____

_____

_____

_____

_____

_____

_____

_____

_____

_____

_____

_____

_____

_____

_____

_____

5. What questions would I ask a seasoned death doula if I had the opportunity, and how could their responses shape my understanding of the role and its impact on individuals and families during the end-of-life journey?

_____
_____
_____
_____
_____
_____
_____
_____
_____
_____
_____
_____
_____
_____
_____
_____
_____
_____
_____
_____
_____
_____
_____
_____
_____

Chapter 10:

Managing and Getting Support

Through the Dying Process

Managing and getting support through the dying process can feel overwhelming, but with the right tools and guidance, you can create a plan that brings clarity and peace of mind. This chapter focuses on practical steps to organize essential information and make arrangements that reflect your or your loved one's wishes. By using the workbook and templates provided, you can ensure that both you and your loved ones are well-prepared for the transition.

Practical Aspects of Preparing for the End of Life

One of the most important aspects of preparing for the end of life is organizing critical information. This includes personal details, such as full name, date of birth, and Social Security number, as well as contact information for key individuals like your attorneys, doctors, and close family members. Having all this information in one place makes it easier for loved ones to manage the affairs of the person who has passed when the time comes.

Compiling and organizing financial information is also crucial. Information regarding credit cards, bank accounts, investments, and any outstanding debts should all be included. This information benefits loved ones when dealing with estates, paying bills, or settling accounts. Family members will need to know who to get in touch with to complete loan payments or make additional payments if the departed has a mortgage or auto loan, for instance. Maintaining an insurance policy filing system is also essential. This includes long-term care, health, and life insurance. People nearing the end of life must ascertain their family's knowledge of their insurance policy, providers, and access methods. It is also useful to make a list of all medications, doses, and medical history to ensure that loved ones and healthcare providers have this necessary information.

Online presence is another crucial factor to take into account. Having many online accounts, such as social media profiles, email accounts, and online banking accounts, is common in today's digital age. Listing login information, including passwords, and giving it to a trusted family member or close friend can help manage the online persona of the person who has passed, including terminating accounts or informing their online network of their death.

Those nearing the end of their lives should think about arranging their advance care directives, power of attorney, and will. In their will, they must specify who should receive their assets and how they want their inheritance to be divided. It is also a good idea to specify the power of attorney so that if they lose their capacity to make choices for themselves, someone else can. Similarly, an advance care directive details the end-of-life care the individual desires and ensures certain decisions align with their wishes, such as being put on life support. When creating these documents, it is essential to seek legal counsel or advice to ensure they are compliant with the laws and regulations of the area the individual is in, as these can differ in different states, territories, and countries.

Having these records organized makes it easier for loved ones to handle the administrative and legal responsibilities that come with a person's death. It is imperative that these documents be kept current and are regularly examined to make sure they reflect the preferences of the person nearing the end of their life. Another crucial factor to think about is the arrangement of personal goods. It can be useful to list valuables, such as jewelry, artwork, and family heirlooms, with the names of those to inherit them. Another option is to gift some of these things to loved ones while still living, making loved ones happy and creating lasting memories.

Individuals nearing the end of their lives can also think about starting a legacy project or memory book containing letters, sayings, advice for loved ones, and mementos and experiences from all the stages of life. Making a remembrance book is a heartfelt and healing approach to leaving a legacy and can console and comfort loved ones long after the individual has passed away.

Ultimately, it is imperative that those facing the end of life have candid discussions about their desires and expectations with their loved ones. These conversations may be challenging, but they are essential to make sure that family members are ready for the practical and emotional issues that come with a loved one's departure and that the individual's desires are honored.

Organizing important personal, financial, legal, and medical information is an essential component of end-of-life preparation as it allows loved ones to be prepared to handle the departed's affairs and the difficult duties that come with a person's death. Taking the time to arrange important documents helps the person nearing the end of life and their loved ones feel more at ease and guarantees that their wishes and legacy are acknowledged and cherished.

Addressing and documenting healthcare preferences is also critical to end-of-life planning as it ensures that wishes regarding medical treatment are respected, even if the person nearing the end of life cannot communicate them. Living wills or advance directives outline medical and end-of-life care preferences, or a healthcare proxy or durable power of attorney can be appointed to make decisions on the individual's behalf. These measures ensure that medical care aligns with the individual's values and desires, even if they cannot express them.

Planning Funeral and Burial Arrangements

Funeral and burial arrangements are also an essential part of end-of-life planning. By specifying preferences for burial or cremation, the type of service, and any specific requests for readings, music, or other elements of the ceremony, the person nearing the end of their relieves their loved ones of the burden of making these decisions during a time of grief. Additionally, setting aside funds or purchasing a funeral plan in advance to cover the costs of funeral and burial arrangements can relieve the burden on loved ones. In addition to guaranteeing that their desires are honored, individuals nearing the end of their lives who take the time to arrange their funeral and burial also provide their loved ones with a sense of relief and closure. For example, consider organizing a memorial ceremony for a loved one who held strong beliefs about music but kept them to themselves. Making decisions on their behalf might be accompanied by a crippling sense of shame and confusion. Having a well-defined plan in place, however, may be a huge relief. For instance, a friend, Abigayl, who passed away a few years ago, had extremely particular tastes in funeral flowers. She also wrote her favorite florist a note outlining her exact preferences for arrangements and colors. Though it may seem like a little matter, knowing that we were carrying out her desires brought her family solace.

Taking cultural and religious customs into account is another crucial component of funeral and burial planning. It's crucial to honor the preferences of those nearing the end of their lives, as they may have valuable rituals or beliefs. In some African societies, for example, it is common to hold a traditional ceremony—which may include certain rituals and ceremonies—to honor the departed. Likewise, there might be certain guidelines for the burial or cremation procedure in various religious traditions.

Those nearing the end of their lives should consider the environmental impact of their funeral and burial plans in addition to cultural and religious issues. An increasing number of people are choosing eco-friendly funeral options, such as natural burial methods or biodegradable coffins, as a result of increased worries about sustainability and climate change. This lessens the impact on the environment and gives bereaved individuals a sense of serenity and comfort.

The psychological and emotional effects of burial and funeral plans on their loved ones should also be taken into account. For example, some people want a more joyful setting with music and laughter, while others might want a more solemn and contemplative ambiance. By better understanding what will comfort and console those left behind, people facing the end of life can plan their funeral and burial to balance their wishes with what will provide their loved ones comfort. Costs are a crucial consideration when it comes to the practical aspects of planning. Those nearing the end of their life may want to think about putting money aside or buying a funeral plan to help with the costs of funeral and burial arrangements, which can be high. When loved ones do not have to deal with these costs, it can provide the individual peace of mind that their affairs are taken care of and their family can focus on bereavement. People nearing the end of their lives should think about how to incorporate their funeral and burial plans into their entire estate plan. This can involve writing down their preferences in a will or other legal instrument or appointing a funeral representative or agent who will be in charge of carrying out their intentions.

Finally, making plans for a funeral and burial is a crucial component of end-of-life preparation. Those nearing the end of their lives can both ensure that their desires are respected and fulfilled and relieve their loved ones of the stress of having to make tough decisions during a time of loss by expressing their preferences in advance. Through careful consideration of the cultural, religious, environmental, emotional, and practical components of funeral and burial planning, people can design a plan that genuinely embodies their values and beliefs.

Self-Reflective Questions

1. How can I navigate my own emotions, fears, and vulnerabilities while providing unwavering support to individuals and families through the dying process, and what strategies can I employ to seek and accept the support I need to maintain my own well-being and resilience in this challenging role?

_____

_____

_____

_____

_____

_____

_____

_____

_____

_____

_____

2. What are the most important aspects of my end-of-life care that I want to ensure are respected and honored, and how can I clearly communicate these wishes to my loved ones and caregivers?

_____

_____

_____

_____

_____

_____

_____

_____

_____

_____

_____

_____

_____

_____

_____

_____

_____

3. How can I gather and organize essential information, such as my medical history, advance care directive, and personal preferences, to ensure that my needs are met and my wishes are respected during the dying process?

_____
_____
_____
_____
_____
_____
_____
_____
_____
_____
_____
_____
_____
_____
_____
_____
_____
_____
_____
_____
_____
_____

4. What kind of support systems do I need to put in place to ensure that my loved ones are cared for and supported during this difficult time, and what resources are available to help them cope with grief and loss?

_____
_____
_____
_____
_____
_____

_____

_____

_____

_____

_____

_____

_____

_____

_____

_____

_____

_____

_____

_____

_____

5. In what ways can I involve my loved ones in the planning process, and how can I ensure that they understand and respect my wishes for my end-of-life care, even if they disagree with them?

_____

_____

_____

_____

_____

_____

_____

_____

_____

_____

_____

_____

_____

_____

_____

_____

_____

Conclusion

As you come to the close of your journey through the complex world of end-of-life care, it's important to consider the major ideas and lessons highlighted by this book. Even though it affects everyone, dying is a very complicated and personal process, encompassing psychological, emotional, spiritual, and medical facets. Comprehending these aspects is essential to offering comprehensive assistance to individuals approaching the end of their life.

The importance of a caring presence and the special function that death doulas play in this delicate process has come up time and time again. Death doulas provide guidance, support, and emotional stability to the dying and their loved ones beyond their role as caregivers. By providing pragmatic aid, psychological consolation, and spiritual direction, they foster an atmosphere in which people can face death with honor and serenity. Death doulas are set apart from other end-of-life care providers by this all-inclusive support system, which highlights their crucial role in promoting a dignified and purposeful dying process.

You have examined a range of topics related to end-of-life care in the chapters, including the issues that occur on an emotional and spiritual level, as well as the physical changes and symptoms related to dying. You learned important lessons about accepting death and celebrating life as you investigated how many nations and traditions see it. To enable a smoother transition for all parties involved, practical aspects have been addressed, such as gathering crucial information and designing tailored end-of-life care plans.

For those inspired by the path of becoming a death doula, this book has provided insights into the necessary training and certification, practical experience, and ethical standards required to excel in this field. The journey of a death doula is one of continuous learning, empathy, and resilience. By cultivating these qualities, aspiring doulas can make a significant impact on the lives of those they serve, offering comfort and guidance during one of life's most challenging times.

Recognizing the importance of self-care for individuals providing end-of-life care is equally crucial. This work has an emotional cost that might result in burnout and compassion fatigue. Maintaining a rewarding and well-balanced practice requires strategies for dealing with these obstacles, developing resilience, and connecting with support systems. Death doulas and caregivers can continue to offer the best care possible with compassion and strength if they put their own well-being first. When seeking support from a death doula, this book serves as a comprehensive guide to understanding the value and services these professionals offer. The real-life examples and testimonials included have illustrated the profound difference a death doula can make in navigating the end-of-life process.

Whether you are facing your own mortality, supporting a loved one, or simply seeking to understand more about end-of-life care, the insights and resources shared here aim to empower and guide you through this inevitable part of life. In the end, it is impossible to overestimate the transformational power of compassionate presence near the end of life. The last moments are sometimes not peaceful. It is, however, a privilege and sacred thing to be part of.

May you be equipped and motivated to approach end-of-life care with courage and compassion as you close these pages. These ideas and expertise will be a great starting point for anyone considering death doula work or seeking help from one. Recall that the dying process is about more than just living your final days; it's also about the deep relationships and experiences that mold our lives and leave behind lasting effects. You respect the essence of what it means to live and die with grace by accepting this journey.

Please give this book a review on Amazon.com if you liked it. I would be very grateful.

Glossary

- **Advance directive:** Legal documents that allow individuals to specify their preferences for medical treatment in the event that they become unable to communicate their wishes. This may include decisions about life-sustaining treatments and end-of-life care.

- **Death doula:** A trained professional who provides nonmedical, holistic support to individuals and their families during the end-of-life process. They offer emotional, spiritual, and practical guidance to help navigate the dying process.

- **End-of-life care:** The medical, emotional, and spiritual care provided to a person in the final stages of life. It focuses on ensuring comfort, dignity, and quality of life for individuals nearing death.

- **Hospice care:** End-of-life care provided by a team of healthcare professionals, volunteers, and family members. Hospice care aims to provide comfort and support to individuals with terminal illnesses in their own homes or in a hospice facility.

- **Palliative care:** Specialized medical care that focuses on providing relief from the symptoms and stress of a serious illness. It is aimed at improving the quality of life for both the patient and their family.

- **Spiritual care:** Support that addresses the spiritual and existential concerns of individuals facing the end of life. It may involve providing comfort, meaning-making, and support for spiritual practices.

Appendix

Workbook on End-of-Life Planning

An end-of-life planner is a comprehensive document or set of documents that contain important information and instructions related to personal, financial, medical, and legal matters to guide your loved ones and ensure your wishes are carried out when you pass away. As discussed in the main book, it's essential to gather and organize important documents, such as a will, power of attorney, advance care directives, and insurance policies. Additionally, consider including funeral arrangements, obituary information, and any specific requests or wishes for your memorial service. Don't forget to update your beneficiaries, and make sure your loved ones know where to find these documents.

As you prepare an end-of-life planner, you also need to solicit legal advice regarding regulations in your state or country. The following workbook ensures comprehensive coverage of end-of-life planning, providing clear guidance and ample space to insert personal details and preferences.

Who Have You Discussed End-of-Life With?

List the people you have discussed your end-of-life wishes with (family members, friends, healthcare professionals):

_____

_____

_____

_____

_____

_____

_____

_____

_____

_____

List prompts for any follow-up conversations needed:

_____

_____

_____

_____

_____

_____

_____

_____

_____

_____

_____

_____

Do You Have an Enduring Power of Attorney?

If you have a power of attorney, record who it is and their contact information:

_____

_____

_____

_____

_____

_____

_____

_____

_____

_____

_____

List the steps on how to set one up if you don't have one:

_____

_____

_____

_____

_____

_____

_____

_____

_____

_____

_____

List any legal considerations and resources for more information:

_____

_____

_____

_____

_____
_____
_____
_____
_____
_____
_____

Special Messages to Family Members

Write your messages to family here:

_____
_____
_____
_____
_____
_____
_____
_____
_____
_____

List prompts to help express thoughts and feelings:

_____
_____
_____
_____
_____
_____
_____
_____
_____
_____

Write personal messages to friends:

_____

_____

_____

_____

_____

_____

_____

_____

_____

_____

Personal Information and Documentation

Checklist of important documents (birth certificate, social security number, insurance policies, etc.):

_____

_____

_____

_____

_____

_____

_____

_____

_____

_____

List the location of these documents:

_____

_____

_____

_____

Contact information for your lawyer, accountant, and other key advisors:

Medical and Healthcare Wishes

Detailed instructions for medical directives and living wills:

Specify your healthcare preferences (DNR, DNI, pain management, etc.):

_____
_____
_____
_____
_____
_____
_____
_____
_____
_____

List information on how to communicate these wishes to your healthcare provider:

_____
_____
_____
_____
_____
_____
_____
_____
_____
_____
_____

Outline your financial assets and liabilities:

_____
_____
_____
_____
_____
_____
_____
_____
_____
_____

Checklist of financial documents (bank accounts, investments, debts, etc.):

_____
_____
_____
_____
_____
_____
_____
_____
_____
_____

List tips for organizing your financial affairs:

_____
_____
_____
_____
_____

_____
_____
_____
_____
_____

Funeral and Burial Preferences

Detail your preferences for your funeral and burial or cremation:

_____
_____
_____
_____
_____
_____
_____
_____
_____

Checklist of funeral service options (music, readings, attendees, etc.):

_____
_____
_____
_____
_____
_____
_____
_____
_____
_____
_____

List information on preplanning and prepaying for funeral services:

_____
_____
_____
_____
_____
_____
_____
_____
_____
_____

Digital Legacy

List instructions on how to manage your digital legacy (social media accounts, email, online banking, etc.):

_____
_____
_____
_____
_____
_____
_____
_____
_____
_____

List usernames, passwords, and instructions for digital assets:

_____
_____
_____
_____

List tips on appointing a digital executor:

_____

_____

_____

_____

_____

_____

_____

_____

_____

_____

_____

_____

Legacy and Memory

Outline any legacy projects or charitable contributions you wish
to make:

_____

_____

_____

_____

_____

_____

_____

_____

_____

_____

List prompts for writing a legacy letter or ethical will:

_____
_____
_____
_____
_____
_____
_____
_____
_____
_____
_____

List suggestions and ideas for creating a memory book or video for loved ones:

_____
_____
_____
_____
_____
_____
_____
_____
_____
_____
_____
_____

Review and Update

Note when you last reviewed and updated your end-of-life plan:

_____

_____

_____

_____

_____

_____

_____

_____

_____

_____

Checklist for regular review intervals (annually, bi-annually, etc.):

_____

_____

_____

_____

_____

_____

_____

_____

_____

_____

_____

Prompts to remind you of key areas to revisit and update as needed:

_____

_____

_____

_____

_____

_____

_____
_____
_____
_____
_____

Remember to keep your end-of-life planner in a secure but accessible location, and inform your loved ones and trusted individuals where they can find it when needed. Regularly review and update your end-of-life planner to ensure that it reflects your current wishes and circumstances. Consulting with legal and financial professionals can also help ensure that your end-of-life plan is comprehensive and legally sound.

References

Aramesh, K. (2016). History of attitudes toward death: a comparative study between Persian and western cultures. *Journal of Medical Ethics and History of Medicine, 9.* https://www.ncbi.nlm.nih.gov/pmc/articles/PMC5432944/

Britannica. (2023). *Death - Hinduism.* Encyclopedia Britannica. https://www.britannica.com/science/death/Hinduism

caregiving.com. (2023). *Understanding the role of end-of-life doulas.* Caregiving.com. https://www.caregiving.com/content/understanding-the-role-of-end-of-life-doulas

Ekore, R., & Lanre-Abass, B. (2016). African cultural concept of death and the idea of advance care directives. *Indian Journal of Palliative Care, 22*(4), 369. https://doi.org/10.4103/0973-1075.191741

National Geographic. (2016, September 28). *Day of the Dead.* Celebrations. https://kids.nationalgeographic.com/celebrations/article/day-of-the-dead#:~:text=The%20holiday%2C%20which%20is%20celebrated

Prichep, D. (2015). Adopting A Buddhist Ritual To Mourn Miscarriage, Abortion. *NPR.org.* https://www.npr.org/2015/08/15/429761386/adopting-a-buddhist-ritual-to-mourn-miscarriage-abortion

Purwanto, Y. K. (2022, March 24). *Ultimate guide to Obon in Japan.* Japan Switch. https://japanswitch.com/ultimate-guide-to-obon-in-japan/

Springhills. (2024). *Are death doulas in demand?* Www.springhills.com. https://www.springhills.com/resources/are-death-doulas-in-demand#:~:text=Death%20doulas%20can%20also%20provid e

University of Bristol. (2023). *Death and dying in Buddhism.* Www.bristol.ac.uk. https://www.bristol.ac.uk/religion/buddhist-centre/projects/bdr/chaplains/online-guide.html#:~:text=Buddhists%20recognise%20that%20there%20is

Woaber. (2022, March 21). *Tibetan sky burial.* I Tibet Travel and Tours. https://itibettravel.com/tibetan-sky-burial/

Wolfelt, A. (2023, December 21). *Why is the funeral ritual important?* Center for Loss & Life Transition. https://www.centerforloss.com/2023/12/funeral-ritual-important/

Image References

Balouriarajesh. (2017). *Cremation-ground-hindu-cremation-4848805/.* [Image]. https://pixabay.com/photos/cremation-ground-hindu-cremation-4848805/

Bergadder. (2013). *Couple-elderly-park-bench-old-114328/.* [Image]. https://pixabay.com/photos/couple-elderly-park-bench-old-114328/

Chepopovich. (2019). *Hinduism-religion-indonesia-8464313/.* [Image]. https://pixabay.com/photos/hinduism-religion-indonesia-8464313/

Chillla70.   (2021).   *Family-beach-people-ocean-6398107/*.   [Image].
    https://pixabay.com/photos/family-beach-people-ocean-
    6398107/

Dan_Park. (2016). *Wedding-flower-floral-marriage-1537147/*. [Image].
    https://pixabay.com/photos/wedding-flower-floral-marriage-
    1537147/

Gaertringen.   (2014).   *Hands-aged-elderly-old-senior-578917/*.   [Image].
    https://pixabay.com/photos/hands-aged-elderly-old-senior-
    578917/

Hudsoncrafted. (2017). *Coffee-glasses-open-book-study-2511065/*. [Image].
    https://pixabay.com/photos/coffee-glasses-open-book-study-
    2511065/

Icsilviu.   (2019).   *People-girls-talking-care-6883634/*.   [Image].
    https://pixabay.com/photos/people-girls-talking-care-
    6883634/

IqbalStock.   (2019).   *Self-care-morning-routine-coffee-6886589/*.   [Image].
    https://pixabay.com/photos/self-care-morning-routine-coffee-
    6886589/

Jarmoluk.   (2014).   *Photos-album-old-photo-album-256889/*.   [Image].
    https://pixabay.com/photos/photos-album-old-photo-album-
    256889/

MiVargof. (2018). *Hands-old-man-people-holding-hands-3964554/*. [Image].
    https://pixabay.com/photos/hands-old-man-people-holding-
    hands-3964554/

Papagnoc.   (2015).   *France-provence-bicycle-lovers-1049333/*.   [Image].
    https://pixabay.com/photos/france-provence-bicycle-lovers-
    1049333/

Pecels. (2016). *Kindle-ereader-tablet-e-reader-1867751/*. [Image]. https://pixabay.com/photos/kindle-ereader-tablet-e-reader-1867751//

Pexels. (2016). *Hands-holding-hands-man-1845334/*. [Image]. https://pixabay.com/photos/couple-hands-holding-hands-man-1845334/

Polifoto. (2020). *Embrace-hug-old-people-solidarity-4788167/*. [Image]. https://pixabay.com/photos/candlelight-faith-candles-3612508/

Sabinevanerp. (2016). *Hands-old-old-age-elderly-2906458/*. [Image]. https://pixabay.com/photos/hands-old-old-age-elderly-2906458/

Surprising_SnapShots. (2019). *People-couple-conversation-talking-8550642/*. [Image]. https://pixabay.com/photos/people-couple-conversation-talking-8550642/

Theminjukim. (2019). *Monk-temple-meditation-buddha-4649046/*. [Image]. https://pixabay.com/photos/monk-temple-meditation-buddha-4649046/

Tiyowprasetyo. (2012). *Counseling-stress-angry-99740/*. [Image]. https://pixabay.com/photos/counseling-stress-angry-99740/

Made in United States
Troutdale, OR
12/29/2024

27385710R10090